PRIORITY ONE

WHAT GOD WANTS

NORM LEWIS

LITERATURE
129 Mobilization Drive
Waynesboro, GA 30830-2047
U.S.A.

Published by
OM Literature
PO Box 1047
Wayneshoro. GA 30830-2047
U.S.A.

ISBN 0-87808-215-8

Scripture quotations, except where noted otherwise, have been taken with permission from *The Holy Bible in The Language of Today, An American Translation,* by William F. Beck (Philadelphia: A.J. Holman Co.), 1976.

Printed in Colombia

TABLE OF CONTENTS

Acknowledgments

My heartfelt thanks to

Annabeth,

without whose loving support and secretarial skills this book would not have been built.

FOREWORD

It is my sincere burden and prayer that people who read this powerful book will do it with an open mind and a contrite heart. I have known Norm Lewis for almost forty years and I know he is a man who has put into practice what he speaks and writes about.

I believe many people today are missing God's will for their lives. This book is going to help some of them to get back on target for God.

What Norm has to say about material possessions is especially important in this day when very few are speaking biblically and forcefully on this subject. May some strong prayers of repentance and faith be prayed by all of us who read this vital message!

I hope, when you have finished reading this book, you will also decide to do something in terms of world evangelism and that many will write to the organizations mentioned in the back of this book for further facts and information. Let's not only read this book, but because we know how God uses the printed page, let's get extra copies and distribute them to our friends.

George Verwer

INTRODUCTION

Priority One: What God Wants

To evangelize the world with God's good news is not an option for the follower of Christ. Nor is it the sole territory of a few idealists who choose to be different. Jesus Christ made worldwide witness the business of every believer. Multiplied millions of lives at stake make this priority one.

The integrity of the Lord Jesus Christ is on the line. He defined the task. He described the life the believer is to live. We who have received Christ as Lord and Savior are accountable to Him. Every Christian will answer at last to Him based on obedience to His command, "Go everywhere in the world and preach the good news to the whole world" (Mk.16:15).

This book tells how I got involved in this matter of highest priority and why I believe it should be the business of every believer.

I felt I had received salvation
and would go to heaven,

but is that the only purpose
of the Christian life?

What does a new believer do?

Attend Bible Study, church,
and prayer meetings, of course.

Follow the commandments, indeed.

But what else?

What is the real goal
of being a Christian?

I felt restless
and confused.

Charles Colson

Chapter One

Getting It Straight

I will never forget that first autumn of pre-med studies at the University of Nebraska. I marched to the same music as the other students. My majors in natural science and literature were a good mix and I liked my classes.

Big Red football mania went wild. Whatever story the score told, we believed our team was best. Our destiny was to be the best.

Besides all that the university offered, I had the outdoors. I loved pursuing rabbits, crows or squirrels; experiences that were pure delight.

Then one evening, I was invited to a preaching service. The message convinced me that if I accepted God's invitation to personally receive His Son, He would forgive my sins and save me. That was the best news I had ever heard! I walked to the front when invited, knelt, and asked Jesus Christ to become my Savior and Lord.

Things changed! For one thing, the Bible read like a new book. The summer before my conversion, I had plodded through the Gospels and part of Acts but quit when I became bored. Now the same pages intrigued me. I carried my New Testament to the University and read snatches between classes searching out the plot. The Gospels and Acts seemed totally new. As I read, I discovered that Christ was commanding believers to offer people everywhere a reasonable chance to know Him. That may not surprise you but it was a moving discovery for me. I imagined myself with the disciples after the resurrection hearing Christ say,

I have been given all power In heaven and on earth ...go and make disciples of all people (Mt.28:18-19).

Did that mean a believer had to be available to go anywhere in the world? Did God intend every Christian to share in His world rescue operation? Those questions hit me head-on with such force that now, years later, I must tell you why I believe that to receive Christ invites radical, personal changes. Ask yourself, "Am I willing for Him to reshape my life? Am I yielded to the lordship of Christ?" The truth is:

God's World Rescue Plan Includes Every Christian

I came to see that God had, indeed, given Christians that task. The big picture was too explicit to be missed. God loves the world; all of it. Have you noticed (as I did) how specific the words of Jesus are? He said that the field is the world, go into all the world, preach the gospel to every creature, you shall be My witnesses to the uttermost part of the world, etc. The believer's responsibility to witness is not limited to his local scene.

I began to sense that the Lord's order to "go and make disciples" might alter my life. To do the work He wanted done could upset plans for normal living. His command required action, and that was an unsettling idea! My sense of the stunning relevance of those facts has deepened across the years, thus I am eager to encourage you to find your part in God's plan for the world.

I believe you will agree that the person who means business with God will do what He wants. That thought struck me again as I came to the end of Mark's gospel and read,

Go everywhere in the world and preach the good news to the whole world. He who believes and is baptized will be saved, but he who doesn't believe will be damned (Mk. 16:15-16).

Those words affirm:

The Christian Must Witness Worldwide

That seemed a large order. What practical effect should that command have on the believer? I remembered hearing that a Christian is the slave of Jesus Christ. If so, the Lord has the right to decide where he will work. I realized that was only the beginning of my struggle when I was confronted with the implications of having said, "My life belongs to Jesus Christ. I've made Him the Lord of my life." I gradually came to comprehend this fact: By accepting Christ's lordship you unlock God's guidance. God says,

I will instruct you and teach you the way you should go. I'll not close My eye on you (Ps. 32:8). Don't be like a horse or a mule without sense; with a bit and bridle their rebellion must be restrained so you can come near them.

An Antidote for Apathy

There came a day when in a west coast church I spoke on "God's World Plan." Afterward a man confronted me with objections. He argued fiercely, "If you knew the terribly deteriorated conditions at Berkeley and other universities, you'd agree we should focus all gospel efforts in those places, not abroad."

I asked him, "But what are our orders, sir? In the first gospel Christ commanded, *'Disciple all nations.'* In the second He ordered, *'Go into all the world and preach the gospel to the whole creation.'* In Luke, *'You will preach to all people.'* In Acts, *'You will testify of Me... to the farthest parts of the world.'* In Romans, *'People Will believe and obey... among all nations.'"*

The man went away shaking his head. Some weeks later, we met again and to my surprise he told me he had been studying the Bible and saw that it does indeed obligate the Christian to witness to all people.

Later I read how the famous missionary, Robert Moffat, after twenty-three years in Africa sailed back to England. He told of his motive for overseas service, saying:

I have tried to look upon those hands and feet streaming with blood. I have tried to look on that thorny crown that encircled the sacred head of the Son of God. I have tried to hear His voice. I have read in the words of eternal truth what He said and I believed He was the Son of God and the Savior of the world. I believed that what He said was true, "Go ye into all the world and preach the gospel to every creature."

Are we asking the Lord, as Moffat did, to give us the true meaning of His command? To read the Bible carefully with such an attitude is apt to destroy complacency.

Pentecost Means Power

Complacency was not a trademark of the early believers and they are our role models. In Acts 1:8, Jesus had told them,

When the Holy Spirit comes on you, you will receive power and will testify of Me in Jerusalem, in all Judea and Samaria, and to the farthest parts of the world.

The Holy Spirit and not a spirit of complacency was given to make Christians effective witnesses worldwide. But like us they were slow to move out. With what result? Compare Acts 1:8 with Acts 8:1 for the answer. The eighth chapter tells of a great persecution unleashed against the Jerusalem church. It scattered all believers except the Apostles throughout Judea and Samaria. Those common Christians *"...went from place to place telling the good news"* (Acts 8:4), but the church leaders remained in Jerusalem!

The fact that those common believers all shared the good news reminds me of an experience in Argentina. We were launching an evangelistic campaign with a street meeting in a place called Capilla del Señor. A sizeable group stood listening when a passing Ford V8 stopped suddenly. A black-robed priest jumped out, ran to a nearby policeman and ordered him to stop us. Failing in that the priest got back in his car and glared at us until we were through. The next day, another believer and I called on the priest at the church house. In his study, we explained we were obeying God's command to go everywhere with the good news. The priest broke in, "That command was to the apostles. It has nothing to do with those not in the apostolic succession!" I asked him to read Acts 8:1 aloud. He read,

That day a great persecution broke out against the church in Jerusalem, and all except the apostles were scattered.... So the people who were scattered went from place to place telling the good news.

The priest saw at once that it was common Christians, not the apostles, who were witnessing. He changed the subject and refused to return to Acts 8.

The Lord let persecution push those believers out to win multitudes they had been neglecting. Since He is the same yesterday, today, and forever, I saw that He might expect me to do that work also. That "impression" changed to "conviction" through a text I came upon while reading the Book of Acts. You may recall how Jesus told his disciples they would receive power when the Holy Spirit came upon them in order to make them effective witnesses "... to the farthest parts of the world (Acts 1:8). Then came Pentecost. Peter assured his listeners,

You will be given the Holy Spirit. What is promised belongs to you, to your children, and to all who are far away, all whom the Lord our God will call (Acts 2:38-39).

That was the text that hit me. I knew God had called me to Himself; therefore, His promise included me. If you are a Christian that promise is to you and for you! What words or language could more powerfully press people into active service for Christ? Another motivating factor is that:

Two Billion Unreached People Face a Hopeless Future

To meditate on that truth brings no pleasure. We wish it weren't so. But the Bible declares that every human being has been distanced from God by sin. He is already condemned (Jn. 3:18,36). God owes no one salvation. He offers it freely, by grace, through His Son. There is no other way (Acts 4:12). All who are not saved through Christ face a hopeless future. Surely every Christian must ponder this. Think of it! Half of humanity is headed for eternal separation from God without even knowing that Christ came to open a way back to God. Whose fault is it that they don't know? Who must bear the blame? Must God?

He didn't send His Son into the world to condemn the world but to save the world through Him (Jn.3:1 7).

The cross proved how much those words meant. We must, however, be open to receive God's full revelation of our role.

Dr. Daniel Bacon, long with Overseas Missionary Fellowship, writes:

The Bible clearly teaches that there are only two destinies open to man (Matt. 13:49-50,25:41; 1 Thess. 1:8-10). . .. most of what we know about eternal judgment and hell came from the same lips that spoke to us of eternal life and heaven. What right have we to accept Jesus' teaching on eternal life and reject what He taught about eternal death? We do not preach the wrath of God because we like to, but because our Lord taught it. The lostness of man is a forceful fact of Scripture. It is a fact which should first drive us to our knees and then into the world.... Let us beware of the Trojan horse of universalism which blinds us to the true state of the non-Christian world and cuts the vital nerve of mission outreach.

Indifference is Incredible

I was appalled at my ability to accept as fact the utter lostness of humanity and yet remain quite apathetic about entire peoples still unreached with God's good news about Christ. I found that many others share this failing. In his book, Confronting Casual Christianity, Dr. Charles Stanley writes:

The severest sin of Christians is a numbing lack of concern, an anesthetized attitude of, "I don't care. I'm in the fold. Why should I concern myself? Is it a wonder people are rushing headlong to perdition? While you read these lines, thousands are perishing, "dead in trespasses and sins."

The practical question therefore is:

What will you and I do to change that situation? Are you available to God? Were you to hear Him say, "Whom shall I send and who will go for us" would you answer, "Here am I, Lord, send me?"

What if thousands of believers from western lands were to migrate to areas beyond present Christian boundaries? That army of heaven's ambassadors could bring multiplied thousands to Christ. But because few Christians care enough to act decisively, the awful waste of souls goes on. Perhaps Dr. Christian Weiss had that in mind when he said,

I am convinced that most Christians have missed the will of God for their lives.

That was nearly the case with me. As a new believer, I learned of Christ's Great Commission and the lostness of those without Him. Did I hurry to get ready to go with the gospel to an unreached people group? The answer is, "No." My selfish plans for my life stood in the way. The battle raged in me until I could say to God, "I want what You want for my life."

In a similar way Gratton Guinness and his wife made mid-course career changes after contact with J. Hudson Taylor from China. Why? In their words:

While millions, tens of millions, hundreds of millions of our fellow creatures are living and dying without ever having heard of a Savior, we ought not to act as if Christendom were the great or even the principal sphere for gospel work....To evangelize among those who are professing Christians already is not to fulfill our Lord's last order, "Go ye into all the world and preach the Gospel to every creature."

Response is Required

Why do Christians so commonly treat Christ's command as something remote from reality? His words ought to form the foundation of our most practical plans. To be guided by His wisdom is to build the life that wins. God asks each to answer His call.

Dr. Ralph Freed, then Director of TransWorld Radio, visited our Christian and Missionary Alliance Church when I was a young pastor. He told us that at age twenty-five, he had a good position with the Burroughs Corporation in Detroit selling custom installations to large businesses. Freed heard the gospel and was saved. As a faithful witness he told his office associates of his faith in Christ. One day a colleague pointed his finger and asked,

"Ralphie, do you really believe all the stuff you've been telling me about salvation and that every man has to accept Christ to get to heaven?"

"Yes," he said, "I believe it with all my heart."

His friend moved closer for a point-blank shot:

"Ralphie, if you believe the heathen in Africa and Asia who have never heard the gospel are hopelessly lost, and you are satisfied to sit in your comfortable office and draw your salary, you are the biggest hypocrite I ever knew!"

That challenge from an unconverted man kept Ralph from sleep that night. He later said:

I was thinking about all the implications of his confrontation. I was very happy at Burroughs. I had a wonderful wife and a baby boy. My life looked successful as it rolled out before me with a promising future. But when I returned to the office the next morning it didn't look the same. The swivel chair didn't seem nearly so comfortable as it had the day before.

In time the Freeds moved out to meet the greater need. For twenty-two years they served in the transjordanian area and in Syria, then helped launch the radio work that became TransWorld Radio. How many lost were saved because the Freeds responded to Christ's clear command!

A convicting question remains. Why should the Freeds' case be uncommon? Why should such a response not be expected'? Is real commitment among believers so rare?

The obedience of a tiny minority cannot offset the sad results of the majority's disobedience. We cannot follow Christ and disregard the work that is so dear to Him. The Bible tells us that a day of reckoning is coming for Christians. Before that hour comes, can we not change our ways?

Yes, we who have received Christ must expect Him to make radical changes in our plans. We must hold our life wholly at His disposal. To do less is unacceptable to Him. He is deeply testing our motives as He told us He would. Ours is the choice to fully follow Him. If we do, we will find that God has a part for each of us in His world rescue plan.

Chapter Two

Costly Contradictions

Death in space came frighteningly close to the crew of the Apollo 13. It was April, 1970. Already two moon landings had been achieved and the world had become accustomed to space flights. Then, the unexpected happened two days into the ten-day mission. An explosion in the service module cut needed energy, fuel and oxygen supplies. The astronauts began a dramatic struggle for life. A stunned world focused on the crippled space ship and thousands began to pray for the men.

The *London Daily Sketch commented*, "God forgive a blase world. We've begun to take the courage of the astronauts for granted." A leftist newspaper in Italy commented emotionally, "Nothing in the cosmos is worth one human life. The moon is nothing but a big stone. Let it go to hell and give us back our three brothers."

What is the worth of a human life? Centuries earlier Jesus had said,

What good will it do you to win the whole world and lose your soul? Or what would you give to buy back your soul?

By His life and death, Jesus showed the supreme value of a soul. His example should change the attitude of his followers conforming it to His own. Let me illustrate what I mean: Albert Einstein was a very intelligent man. When the first atomic explosion occurred Einstein said,

Now everything in the world is changed, except our way of thinking about it.

When Jesus Christ died to pay for the world's sin and rose again Christians could have said, "Now everything in the world is changed, except our way of thinking about it."

The results of Christ's cross and empty tomb are enormous! The implications challenge our whole way of life. Nothing is as it was. All is changed. It is good news and Christ's resurrection has given hope to the human race. God's good news is unique. Nothing compares to it, not even remotely! No one need now face being lost forever. Jesus is the open door into the Father's family, home and heart. *"Whosoever will may come!"* Wow!

We Must Deliver God's Good News

My conversion brought all that to me. I felt vibrant with new life. To know the Lord and stay silent seemed contradictory. How could anyone with God's good news keep quiet? But my ardor soon cooled. Why? Perhaps I was adjusting to the atmosphere around me. Our Christian meetings tended to be routine. The style was sedate. We rarely rose above the tempo of "business as usual" in discussing our duty to get the gospel to all people. We were convinced from the Bible and experience that to know Christ meant life; to miss Him meant death. We agreed *"no other name under heaven"* could save anyone.

The good news we had could mean eternal life for millions, but our actions related more to comfort than commitment. Our modest missionary effort was a good work praised by all, but it wasn't an all-out effort to save multitudes from an awful fate. It reminded me of the phrase, "damned by faint praise." Was our conduct denying our doctrine? A jarring thought!

Do such questions trouble you? Surely our behavior must buttress and confirm our beliefs, but all too often our behavior is counter productive. In this chapter we will note contradictions that cripple truth's advance.

The Bible presents Christians as bearers of good news. We are God's messengers to people *"dead in trespasses and sins."* They must know Him or be lost forever.

People who have received God's good news have also been entrusted with the task of telling others. Even though humanity is distanced from God by sin, the instant anyone believes in Christ he is released from Satan's control and placed under God's. No longer a part of the problem, he is now part of the solution and a member of God's global rescue force.

We Know God's Love For The Lost

Outsiders do not know His love. *"For God so loved the world"* are to them only words that begin one of the Bible's best known verses. The unsaved are unaware of his love. As one hymn puts it,

The love of Jesus, what it is,

None but His loved ones know.

Think for a moment how different life in Christ is from the old way. Hope! Peace! Joy!

This brings us to a contradiction:

We know salvation's time is now, yet we do little to share it worldwide.

This is a costly failure. God gave us eternal life to share. No man can measure the value of Jesus' promise:

I tell\you the truth, If you listen to what I say and believe Him who sent Me, you have everlasting life, and you will not be judged, but you have! come from death to life (Jn. 5:24).

To receive that priceless assurance, and then fail to make every effort to share it has to be an enormous sin.

While doing research for a Ph.D. at the University of Washington, I read documents of the Massachusetts Historical Society in Boston. They told how John Eliot witnessed to the Indians of New England during the mid- seventeenth century. Eliot talked with an old chief who said,

"Seeing the English have been twenty-seven years in this land, why did you never teach us to know God till now? Had you done it sooner we might have known much of God and much sin might have been prevented. But now some of us are grown old in sin."

Eliot answered,

"We do repent that we did not do long ago as now we do."

The language is quaint, but it reveals the same unmet need that marks Christless multitudes today. The Bible invites and warns, saying,

Now is the time when He welcomes us. Now is the time when He saves us (II Cor 6:2).

Are we not repeating the sin of Christians of Eliot's day? Notice, then, a second contradiction:

We enjoy God's pardon ourselves, yet we keep it from unreached peoples.

Such conduct is hard to defend. To give God's good news worldwide depends on us. God pardoned us so we could free others. His pardon removes guilt. Christ's offer to forgive is unique. As Paul said,

Jesus forgives your sins and makes everyone who believes righteous and free from everything from which Moses' law couldn't free you (Acts 13:38-39).

To get God's pardon is the most urgent; need of every person on earth. To offer that opportunity to everyone is the work of all Christians.

Remember, we need not murder unreached people with bombs and bullets in order to destroy them; we only need to neglect them. Just leave them ignorant of Christ's offer of pardon. Let them die as they now live, without hope and without God. That will do it.

Something of a parallel may be seen in events that took place on the Isle of Man off the British coast. During a time of war the governor of the island was found guilty of treason and sentenced to be hanged. While he lay in prison awaiting the execution of his sentence, new evidence was found. It proved the governor was innocent and a pardon was issued. But the pardon fell into the hands of a bitter political enemy. He kept the pardon locked up until the governor had been hanged.

As I read that account I thought of the pardon Christ offers to all. He emphasized His aim saying,

. . I like mercy and not mere sacrifice. I didn't come to call righteous people but sinners (Mt. 9:13).

Christ's pardon gets rid of guilt; nothing else can do so. We know that. Why then do we lock it up? Is it part of our self-centered life style? Whatever the reason, that contradiction is hard to defend because:

We Are God's Channel to Reach All Peoples

God has commissioned saved sinners to call lost sinners to Himself. Paul made a tremendous statement to the Corinthians when he wrote:

But God has done it all. When we were His enemies, through Christ He made us His friends and gave us the work of making friends of enemies. In Christ, God was getting rid of the enmity

between Himself and the people of the world by not counting their sins against them, and He has put into our hands the message how God and men are made friends again. Since God is pleading through us, we are ambassadors for Christ. We ask you for Christ, "Come and be God's friends" (II Cor. 5:18-20),

Notice that Paul affirms, *"We are ambassadors for Christ."* We represent the kingdom of Heaven on earth? Yes. A unique appointment. A giant task.

And another contradiction:

We are Christ's ambassadors, but we don't go.

Our work is to evangelize the world. The One with total authority ordered us to "make disciples of all people" (Mt. 28:19). We have been chosen to offer people eternal life, a privilege angels could covet. We ought to be building bridges of truth to all unreached people groups. Do we treat that as a top priority?

Instead, our prevailing attitude may be highlighted by an incident that occurred during our Civil War. General Stonewall Jackson was moving his troops through Virginia when his army found its progress blocked by a river. Jackson ordered his engineers to take measures needed to provide passage for the artillery and wagons. Wisely, he also called the wagon master to his tent and told him to move the wagon train across the river without delay. The wagon master, worked with rocks, fence rails, and other materials at hand to make a bridge of sorts over which the wagon train and supplies could pass.

At dawn the next morning the wagon master strode up to Jackson's tent and said, "General, the troops are all across the river the way you said."

Jackson asked, "But where are the engineers?"

"Oh, they're over there in their tent drawing pictures and designing the bridge."

Our churches in our land have rivers to cross in order to send an army of witnesses to the 2.7 billion people who have never heard of Jesus Christ. Have we tackled that task? Are we even designing bridges?

The cause which concerns itself to help the neglected half of the human family is not popular. But God's word says, "Speak out for those who can't speak, for the rights of those who are doomed" (Pr. 31:8). Missions is a matter of life or death. It is wrong to use funds for material needs that could carry life to those "dead in sins" (Eph. 2:1).

Few Christians seem to grasp this. New facilities absorb billions of dollars while pioneers for Christ barely survive. Christians are asked to sacrifice far more to build buildings than to offer life abroad. Congregations take on mortgages that cripple missions giving for years. Yet life for unreached peoples hinges on our giving. They cannot wait until new buildings are paid for. Thus the enormous waste of unreached souls goes on. How long, oh Lord!

As Dr. A. B. Simpson put it,

> *"A hundred thousand souls a day,*
> *are passing one by one away,*
> *in Christless guilt and gloom.*
> *Without one ray of hope or light,*
> *with future dark as endless night.*
> *They're passing to their doom."*

A letter from a Missions Committee Chairman says in part:

We recently completed a four million, dollar building. We still owe about three million on the new and old buildings. Steward-

*ship had been low-key until we began our fund drive for this new
building three and one-half years ago. We have recently had to
cut our missions budget by $50,000 to meet debt payments.*

It may be more popular to build buildings than to support
pioneer missionaries, but only they can complete our global task.

I am humbled when I remember my early attitude. My
problem was disobedience. The New Testament convinced
me it was my duty to witness to reach unreached. Did that
make me a missionary? My sorry reply is no. My idea was to
enjoy a home in Lincoln, Nebraska, and be a host to tired
missionaries on furlough.

I lost the sense of God's presence and felt miserable. At
last I sought Him in brokenness and confessed my sin. Then
I was willing to go as He had said.

I came to see that my attitude had been much like that of the
chauffeur who was driving a wealthy couple from the East to
California. In the Nevada desert they got lost. Their car broke
down in an isolated place, off the beaten track. Soon their situation became desperate. The chauffeur spent time under the car
every day, but was not able to get it started. The fierce heat took
its toll until finally the man died, then his wife. Later when a
search party reached the scene, they found the chauffeur still
alive. Why? Every day, under the car, he drank water from the
radiator. But he shared none with his employers. Day by day,
hour by hour they weakened and finally died.

What was the chauffeur's crime? It struck me that he was
simply looking out for himself instead of sharing water with
others soon to die. Could I label him a murderer? Was I not
hoarding the Water of Life, knowing that millions were dying for want of it? I remembered Jesus' words,

.. the water I'll give him will be in him a spring of water bubbling up to everlasting life (Jn. 4:13).

How inconsistent of me! Yes, as surely as God's Word is true, we are Christ's ambassadors but don't go. Few facts could be more condemning.

Still another troubling contradiction is:

We declare the Bible is inspired, but we disobey it.

Eternal hope for lost people is in our hands. The Apostle Paul said,

I must help [l am a debtor] Greeks and non Greeks, the wise and the foolish (Rom. 1:14).

In William R. Newell's commentary on Romans He writes,

In the words "I am debtor," we have the steward's consciousness of being the trusted bearer of tidings of infinite importance directly from heaven.

The Bible tells us that faith in Christ is the only way to life:

If you believe in Him, you're not condemned. But if you don't believe, you're already condemned (Jn. 3:18).

I am the Way, the Truth, and the Life. No one comes to the Father except by Me (Jn. 14:6).

No one else can save us, because in all the world there is only one name given us by which we must be saved (Acts 4:12).

These texts confirm the tragic plight of people who have not received Christ as Savior and Lord. Our hymns hold Christians responsible to tell the lost how to be saved. We sing:

I'll go where You want me to go, dear Lord,

Over mountain and plain and sea.

I'll say what You want me to say, dear Lord,

I'll be what You want me to be.

Promises! Promises! How little they mean. The frightening fate of the unsaved stands out in the song:

Eternal glory is the goal

that awaits the sons of light;

Eternal darkness black as death

for the children of the night.

We sing of our bright hope and we sing about the chilling future the unsaved face: "eternal darkness black as death." But do we care? What are we doing to save them from that horror?" In another hymn we sing,

Far, far away, in sin and darkness dwelling,

Millions of souls forever may be lost.

But does their tragedy stir us to action? Why not? The Bible offers them no hope apart from Christ. How inconsistent for us to call the Bible inspired, then disobey it.

We Can Clear Away Contradictions

We say salvation must be shared at any cost. Yet our selfishness sabotages our response. As the Indians of Equador put it, we "rub out with our elbow what we write with our hand." How can we rid ourselves of these contradictions? Like gallstones which threaten to kill, they must be dissolved and eliminated by obedience.

A man who lived consistently was Dr. R. A. Jaffray, son of the wealthy owner of the Toronto Globe newspaper in Canada. He visited the first church I served as pastor. I can see him now, tall, gaunt, greyheaded, with noble features and piercing eyes; a prince among men. In his youth, Jaffray had turned his back on luxury and ease to spend his life extending Christ's kingdom in the Far East. He became the leader of workers planting churches in several previously unevangelized areas. That work consumed Jaffray's adult years. Administration, travel, writing, publishing, witnessing were vital elements of his service for Christ in the Orient.

At an age when most men retire, Jaffray had a strange dream which powerfully impacted his life. He had just completed a trip for the purpose of extending the work still farther into pioneer areas. He wrote :

I felt I had done my bit, as it were. I could leave the responsibility of the perishing souls I had found on a trip to Borneo and the Celebes to others. But the Lord gave me one of those vivid dreams which leave a deep and lasting impression. It was a horrible dream. I thought I was at home. I was a fugitive fleeing from justice. I thought I had stains of human blood on my hands. It seemed the Lord! Jesus was pursuing me. I was full of fear and running for my life. Pure white snow was on the ground. I stopped and tried to wash the blood stains, the "spots of lost souls" from my hands. I looked around and ran again. I awoke and my first words were, "Lord Jesus, what does this mean? I do not fear You, I am not running away from You. I have no blood stains on my hands. I am washed clean in Your precious blood, writer than snow." At once this Scripture came to my mind, "Son of man, I have made you a watchman. Hear the word at My mouth and give them warning from Me. When I say to the wicked, you shall surely die and you do not give him warning or speak to warn the wicked from his wicked way to save his life, the same wicked man shall die in his iniquity but his blood will I require at your hand" (Ezek. 3:17). These are the blood spots on my hands. The blood of immortal souls is required of me till I do my part to warn them, to pay

*my debt and preach the gospel to them. I must tell it. Woe to me
if I don't tell the good news (I Cor. 9:16).*

Robert Jaffray responded by going on into the Dutch Indies
and opening new pioneer fields for the gospel. He was still at
it when World War II broke out. He was taken prisoner by
the Japanese and finally died in one of their internment camps
in the Celebes. His example reminds us we need not tolerate
contradictions in our conduct. They must go. But how can
they be gotten rid of! The next chapter will show what God
expects us to do.

Chapter Three

God's, "Well Done"

When Christians die they pass into the presence of Jesus Christ. Some hear Him say, *"Well done, good and faithful servant."* We know that because He told us. I think Keith Green, the composer, singer, evangelist, heard those words. Why? Here is my answer.

In Europe, in 1982 God gave him a new vision of the world and its needs. Back in the United States, Keith surprised me by phoning to discuss plans for mobilizing youth for overseas service. I heard his last powerful appeal for world evangelization at Devonshire Downs on June 26th in Los Angeles. A few of us met with Keith and his wife, Melody, a week later and talked strategy and cooperation. Three of our young men from Pasadena accepted Keith's invitation to visit him in Texas. Less than a month later they stood on the edge of his air strip as Keith boarded a plane with eleven friends and roared down the runway. Twenty seconds into the air the plane crashed and burned. All aboard died. Keith left a host of sorrowing friends, yet his life was a huge success, because as Keith learned what God wanted done, he kept obeying the new light God shined on his path.

God asks that we, too, walk in the light that He gives us. Therefore, the question we face is very practical: "What must I do in order to hear God say at last. 'Well done, good and faithful servant'?" Have you ever asked yourself that question? I have.

The Bible tells us that the works we do are *"gold, silver, fine stones, wood, hay or straw,"* and will be tested by fire one day. Works that line up with what God has told us to do are gold, silver, and fine stones. The rest will burn. Why not get into the gold, silver, and fine stones business? Put God's priorities first in your affairs. How many friends of yours are doing that? How many are "on the stretch" for God? How many are paying a price to earn His "Well done"?

I invite you to line up your life with God's plan to offer hope to our lost world. Why? Because:

To Obey Is: Our One Good Option

God will reward those who obey Him. It is also true that those who don't obey Him, won't find His greatest blessing. The Bible has much to say about the importance of obedience. To be saved, to receive the Holy Spirit, to have your prayers answered, those huge blessings are promised the person who does what God wants. The matter becomes quite simple when we note that:

His rescue orders on behalf of a broken world appear early in the Bible. When God called Abraham He told him His plan. God spoke words of amazing significance:

In you all the people in the world will be blessed (Gen. 12:3).

The New Testament explanation of those words is astounding. In Galatians 3:8 we read,

The Bible foresaw that God would make the nations righteous by faith, and long ago He told Abraham the good news: through you all nations will be blessed.

God gave the gospel for the world to Abraham!

Jesus Christ fully implemented God's global plan during His life on earth. Do not miss the precision of His words:

Go, make disciples of all nations; go into all the world and preach the gospel to every creature; the field is the world; forgiveness of sins will be preached to all nations.

God Has Told Us What To Do

Every Christian must respond to His words. In a remarkable passage quoted from the prophet Isaiah, the Apostle Paul reminds us that "each of us will have to give an account of himself to God" (Rom. 14:12). Won't that reckoning focus on the work He has assigned us?

But even when we stray from that work, God mercifully works to bring us back to the assignment. Hebrews points out that:

...our natural fathers used to correct us and we respected them. They corrected us for a short time as it seemed best to them. But He corrects us for our good to have us share His holiness (Heb. 12:9-10).

God appeals to our will, but always leaves the final choice with us. The Christian can obey and help meet the world's vast needs or he can side-step the burden. But selfishness today will mean sorrow tomorrow. To favor selfishness to fail the Lord and later to reap a harvest of regret.

A young mother and five year old son visited a doctor friend. Her spoiled child began acting like an accident about to happen, but his mother made no attempt to restrain him. He soon vanished into the doctor's laboratory. From time to time there came a tinkling sound like glass touching glass, but the mother paid no attention. Finally a louder clatter of bottles sounded. The mother said, "Doctor, I hope you don't mind Johnny playing in there."

"No, not at all," said the doctor gravely, "he'll be quiet when he gets to the poisons."

This bizarre story reminds us that to refuse responsibilty can bring about sad results. The Apostle Paul pointed out that love for Christ produces obedient behavior. He underlined our accountability, saying,

... we try hard to please Him. We must all appear before the judgment seat of Christ, each to receive according to what he has done with his life, whether he has used it for good or evil (2 Cor. 5:9- 10).

Refusal Will Be Costly

The judgment seat of Christ is one meeting for which we must prepare. One day in Argentina, I went to the Bank of the Province of Buenos Aires in the city of Olivos to pay the taxes on a local property. A hundred or more people were already standing in a large hall. After some time an official appeared and read loudly the address of a certain property and the amount of taxes owed. Then he demanded, "Who will pay?" Soon a man stepped forward to square the account. The same process was repeated minutes later, and then again. Each time another debt was announced the question came, "Who will pay?" I thought of the coming day in God's courtroom when Christians will be asked hard questions: "Why were God's commands set aside?" and, "What of people who died unreached with the gospel?" Who will pay? Yes, who will pay?

Your response must be to God's plan, not yours. Christ pointed repeatedly to the whole world as the gospel target. It was Jesus who said,

The field is the world; go into all the world and preach the gospel to every creature; you shall be My witnesses to the uttermost part of the world; this good news of the Kingdom must be preached all over the world so that all nations hear the truth.

Yes, people everywhere must hear the good news. That is why unreached peoples are our priority. To give them our prime attention is simply to obey God. Conversely, disobedience grieves our Lord. Let our hearts be pierced by His rebuke,

Why do you call Me Lord, Lord, but don´t do what I tell you? (Lk. 6:46).

Andrew Stirrett's story is; an example of such obedience to God. Although it is sometimes argued that any profession is equally pleasing to God, Stirrett did not believe that. As a pharmacist in Canada he read the Bible and was convicted of his duty to un-evangelized peoples. He said,

There came up before me most vividly my great sin of omission, my failure to tell those who know not the gospel.

As a result, Stirrett sold his business and went to Africa where he spent forty-one years pioneering for Christ. Men and women similarly motivated have, under God, made great progress in world evangelization during the last nineteen hundred years. But it is too soon to quit. The task is not finished; the work is not done.

His Rules Will Count

One afternoon we were flying to Omaha, Nebraska. As we neared the airport, I saw below us a paved highway which ended abruptly with a raised approach at the edge of the Missouri River. But there was no bridge! Obviously a bridge was planned, but where was it? For some reason the task had been left unfinished. Likewise, though Christianity's expansion across nineteen centuries is marvelous indeed, we dare not stop. We must finish the task.

Suppose a wealthy man were to fly me to Venezuela and from the air point out to me a piece of raw jungle 200 square miles in size, then offer me a contract with all the resources needed to clear the jungle from that land. I accept the job and the owner leaves, promising to return. I tackle the job along with family, friends and hired help. We work hard and make progress. After a time ten, then thirty, then sixty square miles have been cleared and cultivated. We continue to advance until half the jungle has been conquered. But now it's a challenge just to fight weeds in the land under cultivation. Suddenly a rumor reaches us, "The owner is coming back." Everyone redoubles his effort in order to make a good showing. Then someone says, "The half we're cultivating looks pretty nice but what about the jungle we haven't touched? What about the other half?"

That pictures our world today. The United States and many other nations have long been plowed and sown with gospel seed. Of course, they still require care. But we dare not forget the untouched jungle, that half of the world whose soil has never been turned with the gospel plow.

Our duty is to finish what God has given us to do. Every Christian has been called and must be mobilized. The believer who obeys God will win great rewards. We can be well assured that:

God Will Reward Those Who Obey

He values obedience. That is evident in the words of the prophet Samuel:

...to obey is better than to sacrifice, and to listen [to God] than to give the fat of rams (I Sam. 15:22).

The ancient sacrifice was an offering to God. Our obedience means more to Him than any offering we might bring.

Jesus, too, offered strong and tender words on obedience.

If you have My commandments and obey them you love Me. And if you love Me My Father will love you and I will love you and show Myself to you (Jn. 24:21).

If you love Me you'll do what I say and My Father will love you and We will come to you and live with you (Jn. 14:23).

Perhaps you haven't thought of it that way, but obedient Christians are essential to God's plan. As A. W. Tozer said, "The world has been in a state of emergency for 4,000 years." The Christian dare not shut his heart to the ignorance that prevails in pagan lands. He must be about his Father's business. In one of Jesus' last statements He assures us,

Yes, I am coming soon and will have my reward with me to pay everyone according to what he has done (Rev. 22:12).

Obedience Saves

[God] tells us to believe in the name of His Son Jesus Christ (I Jn. 3:23). [He] gives everlasting salvation to all who obey Him (Heb. 5:9). When you look for Me, you will find Me; yes, when you search for Me with all your heart, I will let you find Me, says the Lord (Jer. 29:13-14).

An even more basic element of obedience is to make sure you belong to Christ. Do you? No question is more important and each must answer it for himself. Heart transplants require two elements for success: First, there must be a donor and second the patient's body must accept the heart he receives. Rejection of the transplanted heart means failure. Jesus, as donor long ago gave his life for you and me. But what about the second element?

The Bible says,

To all who welcomed Him, who believe In His name, He gave the power to become God's children (Jn. 1:12).

Be sure you have received Him and know that He has accepted you.

Obedience matters in all that we do. The Bible tells of Naaman the Syrian who came to God's prophet, Elisha, to be healed of his leprosy. With no fanfare he was told,

Go and wash seven times in the Jordan and your flesh will be healthy again and clean (2 Kgs. 5:10).

Naaman turned in a rage and left, but afterward listened to his servants and obeyed. When he did, *"his flesh became clean again."* The point is plain; obedience brought healing. So whether the Bible is talking about salvation, healing, receiving the Holy Spirit, or getting answers to your prayers, obedience counts with God. Great blessing awaits the Christian who determines to obey God.

Obedience wins

Jesus put the matter very forcefully when He said:

Let Me assure you,... every one who gave up his home, brothers or sisters, mother, father, or children, or fields for Me and for the good news, will certainly get a hundred times as much here in, this life: houses, brothers and sisters, mothers and children and fields, with persecutions, and in the coming world everlasting life (Mk. 10:29).

At present we know that some 17,000 people groups have NO church. Polls indicate there may be 40 million born again people in the United States. Even if that figure were cut in half, a base of 20 million Christians remains. Could they not support 17,000 missionaries with a heart for planting churches? If one Christian in 300 would go, four missionaries could be sent to every unreached people group. No wonder it is said that the Church is a sleeping giant and must wake up.

The brightest evidence of God's expanding kingdom results from the work of obedient witnesses overseas. The most thrilling proofs of the gospel's power to bring lives under the lordship of Christ are usually the least known. Such events are taking place *"where the seat of Satan is,"* as the Bible puts it. A good example is contained in a letter from a worker now living among a long neglected people living in part of the Indian subcontinent where it is not prudent to write openly about matters of faith.

The worker says,

There continues to remain an unusual openness among our majority neighbors. A couple of months ago at an inquirers' camp in the northern hills, a number of men made commitments and immediately eight were given "a bath!"

Believers who seek baptism are welcome fruit. Similar triumphs are being won in many parts of God's harvest field today. By such cross-cultural demonstration of the gospel's power, God's kingdom continues to push back spiritual darkness.

The exciting fact is that each of us can have his God-given part in evangelizing the world. Ask yourself, "What am I really living for?"

I recently met a friend who is a skilled welder and worker in wrought iron. I asked him what he had been doing lately.

He said, "For the last couple of months I have been working full-time building floats for the Rose Parade.

"That's seasonal work isn't it?" I said

"Not really," he replied. "There's a company I could work for year-round building floats, but I don't want to."

"Why not"

"Because," he said, "all my work on floats is in the Pasadena City Dump."

Then he added, "At choir practice one of my friends who works for a high tech company heard me say that. He remarked, 'All my work is floating around in outer space.' At that a sales lady for Avon beauty products who was standing near us said, 'All my work is down the drain!'"

Their work was gone. "To the dump!" "In outer space!" "Down the drain." Yes, the work many people do to "make a living" is very temporary. But the one who works to give people eternal life will see his work shining in redeemed faces throughout the ages.

To obediently do the work God has given us is the way to hear Him say at last, *"Well done!"* What that work is will become clear in the next chapters as we examine bedrock facts.

Chapter Four

Why Jesus Came

A man went to a pastor for counseling and was asked explain his problem. He said, "My difficulty is the ninth cha ter of Romans where it says, *'Jacob have I loved but Esau have I hated.'*"

"Yes, there is great difficulty in that verse," the pastor admitted, "but which part of it troubles you?"

"The latter part, of course. I can't understand why God should hate Esau."

"The verse has also been a difficulty to me," said the pastor, "but my difficulty has always been the first part of the verse. I never could understand how God could love that d ceiving, scheming scoundrel Jacob."

God's love for us sinners is indeed a mystery, yet true.

Have you ever asked yourself exactly why Jesus came to our world? Fortunately He answers that question for us. In Luke 19:10 He says that He came *"...to look for and save the lost.* But what does "lost" mean?

In the book of Romans the Holy Spirit shows how profoundly "lost" humanity is. We are told that *"all have sinned and are without God's glory"* and that *"Sin pays off with death" (Rom. 3:23; 6:23).* In an awesome summary statement, the Apostle Paul says,

One man brought sin into the world and his sin brought death. And so because all have sinned, death spread to all people (Rom. 5:12).

God's Love Seeks Sinners Worldwide

As a young Christian, I weighed the words concerning the spiritual plight of all people against the notion I had heard that those without the gospel are all right as they are. Not so! The Bible does not teach that everybody will somehow be saved. I remembered the warning so close to John 3:16,

If you believe in Him, you're not condemned. But if you don't believe, you're already condemned because you don't believe ... (Jn. 3:18).

To discover humanity's deadly problem made me want to be a part of God's purpose to save people. Will you join me in that effort? Christ has made plain that He came to earth to seek and to save the lost. To explore that theme is our aim in this chapter.

God gives us a sense of worth by His long-range purpose to offer salvation to lost people everywhere. The Bible declares beyond a doubt that.

Why is John 3:16 the best known verse in the Bible? Because it reveals humanity's darkest danger and brightest hope. The danger is that man could "perish," the hope is that he may *"have everlasting life."* Note it well,

God so loved the world that He gave His only begotten Son so that whoever believes in Him might not perish but have everlasting life.

Sin casts a dark shadow even over the Bible's brightest text.

God's love for the world has no easy explanation. We may assume He should love us, but why? The proof of His love flows through the life and death of Jesus Christ. He was as human as any man. He grew as we do. He worked, wept, prayed and loved. He was tempted in every way as we are, but never sinned. Christ was touched with compassion whenever He saw the confused multitudes wandering like sheep without a shepherd. His love reached out to all humanity. He said,

The field is the world... Go into all the world and tell the good news to everyone.

But He did more than tell God's good news. He died the cruel death of the cross in order that there might be good news to tell. He was unique in what He said and did.

Christ offers Light for Darkness

But how? He said, *"I am the light of the world."* You might think all people would have flocked to Christ, drawn by His radiant life. Sadly, it was not so. One of the Bible's most revealing texts says,

This is why people are condemned: The Light came into the world but people have loved darkness instead of the Light because they have been doing wrong (Jn.3:19).

Sin-hardened people hated the light they saw in Christ and determined to destroy Him. When at last they nailed Him to the cross they thought they had put out the light. But no, His light had already passed into other lives. He had told His followers, *"You are the light of the world"* (Matt. 5:14)

God's Light Shines in Believers

Saved lives are God's lights. Nothing created is more wholesome than light. The Apostle Paul wanted the Christians at Ephesus to radiate goodness. He told them,

Once you were darkness, but now you are light In the Lord. Live as children of light, since light produces every-thing good and righteous and true (Eph. 5:8-9).

Electric lights are marvelous. One company has perfected a light bulb with a life expectancy of a million hours. Think of a bulb shining brightly eight hours a day every day for over 342 years! During its lifetime the bulb will be capable of giving out 286,000,000 lumens (or units of light). But spiritual light through Christ is even more wonderful.

Consider the impact of Christ's words, *"You are the light of the world."* Only sin can dim or destroy Christ's light in a believer. I read of a bad accident at a railroad crossing that produced a bitter lawsuit. The flagman was brought into court and questioned closely as to whether at the time of the accident he was at his post swinging his lantern. He said, "I was there, and I was waving my lantern." Later he confided to a friend, "What scared me most was that they might ask me if my lantern was lit." When Christians' lives are darkened by sin, the forces of evil are unleashed. God intends believers to illuminate the whole world. Their failure to do so is devastating among those peoples whose darkness has never been dispelled by Christ's light.

God's Light Must Shine Worldwide

God's target through us is everyone. Because all without Christ are lost, our goal is to cause gospel light to penetrate every dark corner of earth.

A traveler in the French village of Doubs on a Sunday evening saw people hurrying through the streets to the church, each carrying a lamp. He was told, "We have no other way of lighting the church. When it was built in 1550, the village mayor decided that each member should bring his own lamp. Everyone goes there to make it brighter for he knows if he stays away the church will be darker and the service sadder." Entering the church, the visitor saw on every pew a place to hang a lighted lamp. As people kept arriving the glow from the lamps became brighter and brighter. Light in the church is beautiful, but the world's greatest need is light in its darkest places.

During our bitter American Civil War there were months during which the final outcome was uncertain. At one time a group of men seeking peace gained an audience with President Lincoln. They presented their plan by laying on the desk in front of the President a large map showing the United States and the relative positions of the warring armies. They proposed that the war should cease and that North and South should retain control under separate governments of the territories they then held. When they had finished speaking President Lincoln rose from his chair. He leaned over the map, spread his large hands over it and said, "Gentlemen, this government must have all, all or none."

The God of heaven will never settle for a divided world in which thousands of people groups remain in darkness because we have kept from them the light of the gospel. God is committed to complete His plan in which Christians are the *"light of the world."* Why? Because God loves the whole world:

Christ Offers Life for Death

Christ was explicit about His purpose and His power to achieve it. How startled His hearers must have been when they heard Him say,

Let me assure you, the hour is coming and is here now, when the dead will hear God's Son calling them, and those who hear Him will live. As the Father has life in Himself, so He has given the Son, the power to have life in Himself (Jn. 5:25-26).

Those who respond to the call of God's Son receive light and radiate light in earth's darkness.

During the last world war, an American mother received a very special letter. It was written in her son's familiar handwriting under the heading "Somewhere in the South Pacific."

Dear Mom,

It is comparatively quiet where I am today, but no one knows how long it will be. If this letter reaches you, it will mean that I can't write another one, for I'm putting this away with my things, and asking that it be sent to you. I just want to say, Mom, don't grieve for me. I Know that my Redeemer lives. My trust is in Him who loved me, and gave Himself for me. And because He lives, I too shall live. Don't ever say of me, He's gone. Say, He lives! Because, Mom, when you read this, I shall be very much alive, and waiting for you in Christ's presence.

With love,

John

The letter was read through blinding tears. But in the darkest hour of a mother's life, she was at last able to say, "This really is good news. He lives, he is waiting in Christ's presence.

Eternal Life is Beyond Comparison

How urgent is the need to point every people group to the Door through which that soldier passed from darkness to light. That is why we must go with life wherever death rules. There is no message like the gospel for sinful humanity. No one on earth merits the mercy of God. The very nature of mercy demands that it be undeserved.

A small boy said to his mother that if he could say what he would like to God it would be, "Dear God, love me when I'm naughty." That cry voices the need of every human heart.

People the world over are separated from God by their sin. And, neglected people groups do not know the way to the Father's heart.

To the Christians at Rome Paul directed questions which pointed out the core of the problem. He asked,

But how can they call on Him if they haven't believed in Him? How can they believe in Him if they haven't heard of Him? How can they hear if nobody preaches? (Rom. 10:14).

His conclusion is that witnesses must be sent everywhere. All peoples must be told of Christ's love.

Notice how Christ pictured the Father's love for the lost in the story of the prodigal son. The ungrateful son asks for his inheritance and leaves for the far country. There he wastes his inheritance and his health in riotous living. When he finally "bottoms out," starving, he remembers the abundance at his far-off home. He repents, struggles home and tells his father,

I've sinned against heaven and against you. I don't deserve to be called your son anymore. Make me one of your hired men (Lk.15:19).

Instead, the father has slaves bring the best robe for him, puts a ring on his finger, shoes on his feet, and orders a celebration, saying,

This son of mine was dead and is alive. He was lost and is found,

That is a picture of the Father's heart toward the many people groups still locked in the darkness of their sin and alienation from God.

The British publication, Punch, once ran a cartoon showing a late model car whose occupants were staring at a large sign on a church lawn which read.

For the man who has everything-
EVERLASTING LIFE.
Come inside for full details.

You will agree that everlasting life is so valuable it eclipses the worth of lesser things. Nothing we could take to any people would be comparable to new life in Christ.

I remember a phone call I received in Argentina one day from the unsaved husband of a woman member of our church. He asked me to come at once to a certain hospital. When I got there he grabbed my arm and gasped, "Have they told you about my wife?"

"Yes, they have told me."

"There's nothing to do," he continued, "she is full of cancer. They started to operate, then simply closed the incision." He paused, then added, "This is the worst thing that could happen to us."

I said, "Mr. Rossi, I am more sorry for you than for your wife." He looked at me with surprise. "Yes," I said "you are unsaved, she knows Christ. Thus it is well with her now and forever."

We walked to the room where his wife lay in weakness, her face calm with the peace of heaven. I thought of a Bible verse I had read that morning, "Let the peace of Christ rule in your hearts." Mr. Rossi lacked that peace. Living without Christ, his need was far greater than his wife's even though she was dying of cancer. She knew she would soon be in heaven in the home Christ promised he would prepare for His own.

Eternal Life is of Ultimate Importance

Helmut Thielicke, a man whose preaching stirred many in Germany after World War II, wrote a book called, "Encounter With Spurgeon." Spurgeon, the prince of preachers at the end of the last century when preaching was unpopular, when humanism and modernism were at the peak of their influence, when theology was thought to be superstition had a congregation of 6,000 every Sunday morning in London. And every Monday Spurgeon's whole sermon was cabled to the United States and printed in American newspapers. Thielicke wrote:

It was not the aim of his preaching to show people that their lives would be easier if they accepted the gospel; that it would solve their problems; that civilization would perish without Christianity; that the State and society need religion; etc... All this is a kind of high-minded Christian pragmatism which we are all too prone to promote these days... All this is completely alien to Spurgeon. He is concerned only with salvation. For us and our kind of Christian social ethic, the threatening danger is that we tend merely to explain Christian ideas concerning the world order, the structuring of society, etc., and then to recommend them for their preservative and productive power But since it is possible to have the Christian ideas without actually believing, and to be taken up with the social teachings of Christianity without becoming engaged personally, these ideas lose their connection with the Lord of Christianity and degenerate into ideologies ... Spurgeon dares to say that what really and ultimately counts is to save sinners. Indeed what really counts is that we get to Heaven. Anything else is watered-down social gospel, including all the talk about the Christian West.

The Bible makes abundantly plain that Christ came to save sinners. For us to make that gracious offer known to everyone everywhere is our prime task. It is so important that all other enterprises, by comparison, are insignificant.

A Chinese Christian leader, C. K. Lee, spoke to an American audience and afterward invited questions. He gave a memorable answer to a student who asked,

"Why should we send Christianity to China when it has Confucianism?"

Mr. Lee said,

There are three reasons. First of all, Confucius was a teacher and Christ is a Savior. China needs a Savior more than she needs a teacher. In the second place, Confucius is dead and Christ is alive. China needs a living Savior. In the third place, Confucius is one day going to stand before Christ and be judged by Him. China needs to know Christ as Savior before she meets Him as Judge.

What C. K. Lee summarized so well can help us remember God's long-range purpose to offer salvation to all and to save eternally all who will put their trust in Christ alone. There is no brighter reality than that God loves the whole world. His love seeks sinners worldwide.

Chapter Five

God's Non-Negotiable Purpose

Foundations are important. In the city of Anchorage, Alaska, I saw buildings that had dropped thirty feet in an earthquake.

Anchoring the foundations of New York's skyscrapers was a builder's dream. Under them was immovable bedrock, but building skyscrapers in Chicago was very different. Foundations there had to be secured on the marshy soil at the south end of Lake Michigan.

On what kind of foundation does God's redemptive plan rest? We have seen that He aims to offer all people everywhere a place in His kingdom. Both the Old and New Testaments confirm that purpose.

Perhaps you have struggled with unbelief, as I have, in seeking God's design, His long-range plan for the world. If so, I understand. You want to know the divine purpose. One thing the Bible makes quite clear is that.

Job's life is a classic case of faith that did not fail. He had a tough, bruising time in his battle to trust God. On front center stage he fought to survive.

The drama involved both God and Satan behind the scenes. Hard experience brought Job at last to the right conclusion. Confronted by God he confessed,

I know You can do everything, and nothing You plan is too hard for You (Job 42:2).

Job learned what we all need to understand that:

God Has a
Changeless Plan

As Paul explained to the Ephesians,

He has done what in His kindness He planned to do: before He made the world He who loved us appointed us to be made His sons by Jesus Christ (Eph 1:4).

In reading the Bible it is comforting to observe God's care for people. Adam and Eve had no sooner gotten into trouble through the Devil's deceit than God came looking for them. As the Bible puts it,

At the time of day when there was a breeze, they heard the Lord God walking in the garden, and the man and his wife hid from the Lord God among the trees in the garden (Gen. 3:8).

Adam and Eve were not quick to cooperate with God. Nevertheless, God told the Devil he would be defeated in his attempt to destroy humanity. Eve's "Descendant," Christ, would deliver the deathblow.

He will crush your head, and you will bruise His heel (Gen. 3:15).

God Revealed His Purpose

This fact underlies the Bible's whole message. Chapters one to eleven are introductory: an overview of creation, man's fall, with just a hint of God's plan to redeem us. In chapter twelve, we see the plan take shape. God acted to restore our fallen race. In Genesis 12:3, we read how He revealed His redemptive plan to Abraham, saying,

...*in you all the people in the world will be blessed (Gen. 12:3).*

He reconfirmed that promise with the words,

... *Abraham is bound to become a great and mighty nation and in him all the people in the world will be blessed (Gen. 18:18).*

In your Descendant all the people on earth will be blessed because you did what I told you (Gen. 22:18).

To Isaac, Abraham's famous son, God said,

... *in your Descendant all the nations of the earth will be blessed (Gen. 26:4).*

Once again He revealed His world purpose to Jacob (Gen. 28:14). God made His priority plain to the patriarchs of Israel.

Notice that these statements convey giant-sized good news. Sin had brought God's curse on all humanity. Yet God now says repeatedly that everyone in the world will be blessed. Ask yourself, "What blessing would be meaningful to lost humanity, distanced from God by sin? What could compare with God's offer of salvation by grace through faith?"

God Gave Abraham the Gospel

You may think this too good to be true; that we are reading something into the text. But the New Testament confirms it. The Holy Spirit identifies the promised blessing Abraham, saying,

The Bible foresaw that God would make the nations righteous by faith, and long ago He told Abraham the good news: through you all the nations will be blessed (Gal. 3:8).

God gave Abraham the gospel of salvation through Christ. Patiently, persistently, He presented His plan for world re-

demption to each of the Jewish patriarchs. Jesus reinforces
that tremendous truth with the words,

Your father Abraham was delighted to know of My day;
he saw it and was glad (Jn. 8:56).

Israel was to be God's special witness to the rest of the
world. But in this she failed. Had Israel's leaders put God's
work first, the rest of the Old Testament would have been
different. But despite God's giving them His plan of salvation for all people, those early believers favored their own
affairs.

How like them we are! Then, as now, God's good news
was soon submerged in a sea of human selfishness. As we
move across the ocean of Old Testament history only an oc-
casional island protrudes words of a psalmist or a prophet
reaffirming God's unchanging aim to redeem our fallen race.
What inspiration flashes from those insights! Through the
ages, people sensitive to God have shared in His plan.

Christ Made the Gospel Possible

How wonderful that God chose to appeal to us by His
love instead of by the pressure of His power. He knows
what we are slow to learn, that the only permanent persuasion is that based on love. Man's way of persuasion is often
clumsy.

A company president reprimanded a department head because one of his men was refusing to sign up for a company
plan. The department head called the offender into his office
and tongue-lashed him with abusive words and threats. As
soon as the bellowing stopped the workman signed the form.
The boss asked, "Why didn't you sign up before?"

Wryly the man said, "Nobody explained it to me like that
before."

To force agreement is man's way, not God's. Christ came to earth to prove God's unconditional love for us. Paul says,

In Christ, God was getting rid of' the enmity between Himself and the people of the world by not counting their sins against them, and He has put into our hands the message how God and man are made friends again (II Cor 5:19).

It was hard for the religious crowd in Jesus' day to understand His love for ordinary people. Their highest values included rank, prestige and power. They prejudged Jesus with their question to His disciples, "Why does your Teacher eat with tax collectors and sinners?" Jesus heard them and said,

Those who are healthy don't need a doctor, but the sick. Go and learn what this means: I like mercy and not mere sacrifice. I didn't come to call righteous people, but sinners (Matt. 9:11-13).

Although Jesus frequently healed peoples' bodies, His ceaseless concern was to save them from the power of sin. He literally fulfilled the angel's prophecy made before His birth,

.. you will call Him Jesus, because He will save His people from their sins (Matt. 1:21)

Sin is the basic human problem. That reality became a conviction deeply held by Kier Hardie who led the Labor party in England for thirty-three years. At the close of his career, he said:

If I had to live my time over again, I would give all my strength to preaching the gospel. My social work has not drawn the people any nearer to an appreciation of the gospel. If all my life effort had been put on the side of the gospel, what a different story it might have been as to the eternal well-being of many souls.

Because of the preeminent importance of the gospel in relation to any human scheme or plan, we can understand why:

God Sustains Those
Who Support His Purpose

Though God loved Israel, He never allowed His care of that nation to limit His larger redemptive plan. We see this in His promise concerning Messiah,

It is not enough that You're My Servant to raise the tribes of Jacob and bring back those in Israel who have been preserved, I have also made You a Light for the nations that My salvation might reach to the most distant parts of the world (Isa. 49:6).

Elsewhere He strengthened Isaiah In His rugged prophetic role, saying,

No weapon forged against you will succeed. You will also condemn every tongue that brings an accusation against you. This is the heritage of the Lord's servants: I give them their righteousness, says the Lord (Isa. 54:17).

When God called Jeremiah their dialogue came to a similar conclusion. The prophet argued:

O Lord God!. . . I don't know how to talk. I'm too young. "Don't say, 'I'm too young,'" the Lord told me. "You will go to all I will send you to, and say everything I order you to say. Don't be afraid of them. I'm with you to rescue you," said the Lord (Jer. 1:6-8).

God's directive closes with the words,

They will fight against you but will win no victory over you, because I'm with you to rescue you. This is what the Lord says (Jer. 1:19).

With such divine support there is reason to affirm, One plus God is a majority!

God's Commitment Is Forever

The prophet Baalam, though doomed by his mixed motives, testified to the divine integrity saying,

God is not a man who lies or a mortal who changes His mind. When He says something will He not do it? When He promises, will He not Keep it? (Num. 23:19).

God will achieve His objectives. He will not alter His eternal purpose. Samuel the prophet emphasized that fact to disobedient Saul when he declared,

Moreover, the Glory of Israel does not lie or change His mind because He is not a man that He should change His mind" (I Sam. 15:29).

Many other Bible statements affirm the persistence of God in His redemptive plan. His patience is noteworthy in building similar determination into those who desire to please Him.

Abraham may lie to Pharaoh and fail as a missionary, but God will build his faltering faith. It will in time become rugged enough to inspire people in latter ages who read:

He staggered not at the promise of God through unbelief but was strong in faith, giving glory to God; and being fully persuaded that, what He had promised, He was able also to perform (Rom. 4:20-21 KJV).

Jonah may flee from his divine call, but God will bring him back to the appointed task. Peter may try to kill the high priest's servant with a sword, then cravenly deny his Lord, but one look from the Savior will subdue him in penitential tears. John Mark may desert Paul and seem to be a spiritual discard but God will restore him with distinction.

The prophet Daniel early in life *"purposed in his heart"* (Dan. 1:8 KJV). His desire was to please God and under-

stand what He was doing in the world. Those motives pro-
pelled him into a career without parallel. Daniel started as
a slave in a pagan society. With unfaltering faith he
mounted from one position to another. Surrounded by in-
dulgent, self-serving men, Daniel's character could not be
concealed. His bright star spanned the reign of three kings.
No wonder Daniel has inspired thousands from that remote time to the present. He learned God's plan and moved
with Him.

Countless other weak people have become strong by
choosing God's way. They tested God's promises to protect
and prosper His people. Nor is His guarantee for this life
only. It Spans time and eternity. The Lord Jesus made this
clear when He said to His followers,

*...My friends, don't be afraid of those who kill the body
and then can't do any more. I will point out the One you must
fear. Fear Him who after killing you has the power to throw
you into hell. Yes, I tell you, fear Him! (Lk. 12:4-5).*

Those who embrace God's purpose put themselves beyond the reach of any alien power to permanently hurt them.
Therefore, dogged work to reach God's goals is wise. Our
strength is in Him. Christ's path from Bethlehem to Calvary
was unswerving. He set His face like a flint to go to Jerusalem. He said,

*My meat is to do the will of Him that sent Me, and to
finish His work (Jn. 4:34 KJV). I must work the works of
Him that sent Me while it is yet day (Jn. 9:4 KJV). [Father,]
I have glorified You on earth by finishing the work You gave
Me to do (Jn. 17:4).*

On the cross, completing our redemption, He cried out,
"It is finished" (Jn. 19:30). We too should be goal oriented.

Think of how sinners opposed Him and He endured it. It will help you not to get tired anal give up (Heb.12:3)

The river of God's purpose is freighted with eternal consequences. From its headwaters in the timeless past, it flows through both Testaments. Christ specifically taught His disciples its broad scope:

Then He opened their minds to understand the Bible. "This, "He told them," is what is written: The promised Christ will suffer, rise from the dead on the third day, and in His name you will preach to all people, beginning at Jerusalem that they repent of their sins so that they will be forgiven (Lk: 24:45-47).

Our Lord showed that His death, resurrection and global plan fulfilled Old Testament prophecies. That fact gives huge significance to the world evangelism enterprise.

Our Commitment Is For Life

It was a great day in history when Columbus and his men sailed into the mouth of the Orinoco River. The force of its current carries fresh water far out to sea. Someone suggested they had discovered an island. "No," said Columbus, "This is no island. This mighty current drains the waters of a continent." Similarly, with world evangelization, the Bible outflow of God's good news carries the message of His love for the lost from the headwaters of eternity.

Dr. G. Christian Weiss, who invested his life for God in global evangelism, said:

That which actually makes Christian men and women become genuine missionaries is their arrival at certain convictions from the Bible regarding God's world plan and their Christian responsibility toward the world according to that plan. These convictions drive them to the mission field in the first place and keep them on the field year after year in faithful, selfless service. The mere spirit of adventure or philanthropy is not sufficient to do this. But an understanding of the teaching of Scripture and the sound conviction of its demands on believers will not allow the missionary to do otherwise.

Only people who put their roots down into the rich soil of the Bible will tap ultimate strength. Such people discover the direction God is moving and walk with Him. Nothing can deny them the blessing of commitment to God in pursuit of His goals.

May we be as persistent as the small burro owned by two Texas cowpunchers. They took it with them to the mountain range to bring in a wild steer. Now a big three-year-old steer that's been running loose in the timber is a tough customer to handle. But those cowboys had the technique. They got a rope on the steer and then tied him neck and neck, right up close, to the burro. When they let go, the burro had a bad time. The steer threw him all over the place, banged him against trees, rocks and into bushes. Time after time, they both fell down. But there was one big difference between the burro and the steer. The burro had the idea that he wanted to go home. He had a goal. Every time the steer threw him down, the burro got up and took a step nearer the corral. This went on till about a week later, the burro showed up at the ranch headquarters. With him was the tamest, sorriest looking steer you ever saw.

Although our effort in God's plan may seem ineffective, He will persist until final victory is won. Let nothing rob you of the part He has for you in His worldwide rescue operation. God will guide every believer who stays available to Him. His eye will guide you step-by-step along the path He chooses for you. He wants to bless you in the fulfillment of His plan. Your persistence in world evangelization pleases Him.

Chapter Six

Christ's Sure Return

In the first World War a squad of soldiers left their trench to probe no-man's-land. Caught in enemy gunfire, all but one made it back to the trench. One of the men begged permission to go back for his buddy.

"No," said the sergeant, "he's probably dead and you'll get killed if you go."

The soldier insisted; went out and got his buddy. When he staggered back into the trench his buddy was dead and he was mortally wounded. The sergeant said, "See, I told you not to go. He's dead, and now you're dying."

"No sir," said the soldier. "He was still alive when I got to him and he said, 'I knew you would come.'"

Integrity! Our Lord's return is as sure as His word is true. C. H. Spurgeon, the great English preacher, spoke of Christ's coming again, saying:

I do not find many souls have been converted to God by exquisite dissertations about the battle of Armageddon, and all those other fine things. I have no doubt prophesyings are very profitable, but I rather question whether they are so profitable to the hearers as they may be to the preachers and publishers.

After that touch of humor Spurgeon added,

I do not know the future and I shall not pretend to know. But I do preach this because I know it, that Christ will come for He says so in a hundred different passages.

One day our Lord Jesus said to his followers.

"You, too, get ready, because the Son of Man is coming when you don't expect Him." "Lord," Peter asked, "by this illustration do you mean to warn us, or everybody else too?" The Lord asked, "Who do you suppose is the manager that can be trusted and has good sense, whom the master will put in charge of his servants to give them their share of food at the right time? Blessed is that slave whom his master will find doing just this when he comes. I tell you he certainly will make him manager of all his property.

"But if that slave says to himself, 'My master isn't coming back for some time,' and starts to beat the other slaves, men and women, and eats, drinks, and gets drunk, the master of that slave will come one day when he's not expecting him and at a time he doesn't know and will cut him in pieces and put him with the unfaithful. That slave who knew what his master wanted and didn't prepare himself or do what he wanted will get many blows. But he who didn't know and did things for which he deserved to be beaten will get few blows. If you were given much, much will be expected of you, and if much was entrusted to you, all the more will be demanded of you" (Lk. 12:40-48).

I have quoted at length this teaching of Christ because it focuses sharply on His return. We trust His word, we know He is coming. In this chapter we want to learn how best to serve Christ in that light. God's prophetic calendar should energize our commitment. The New Testament is rich with references to His return. We are accountable to Christ and He exhorts us to be ready for that hour.

Should not each believer be a better ambassador for Christ knowing He is coming? As a matter of fact:

To Know Christ Will Come is Better Than Gold

Why? Gold won't help one's standing with Christ when He comes. But people who know they may face their Lord any moment are moved to work for Him. When D.L. Moody, the mighty soul winner, was asked the secret of his power he said,

I preached for years with the thought that before every sermon was finished the Lord might come.

Dr. G. Campbell Morgan, peerless British Bible expositor, said,

I never lay my head on my pillow without thinking that before morning breaks the final morning may have dawned.

Dr. R. A. Torrey, a scholar and evangelist of immense influence, said,

The truth of our Lord's return is the most precious truth the Bible contains.

George Mueller, famous founder of orphanages, said that when God revealed to him the truth of the personal return of the Lord Jesus,

From my inmost soul I was stirred up to a feeling of compassion for sinners, for the slumbering world around about me.

J. Hudson Taylor, pioneer in China for Christ, said,

This truth of the Lord's return has been the greatest spur to me in service.

Dr. J. Wilbur Chapman, powerful Presbyterian evangelist, said,

I preached the Lords return because the thought of His second coming has changed my whole ministry.

How vital, then, that we be fully alive to the meaning of that amazing event. Jesus Christ is coming back again! Lovingly, before the event:

Christ Reveals Our Part

The New Testament makes it clear that being a Christian involves responsibility. Christ once told of the conduct of three workers in their master's absence. When he returned two were commended while one was condemned (Matt. 25:14-30). Jesus also told of seed sowed on different kinds of ground. He warned,

Be careful, then, how you listen! If you have something, you'll be given more. But if you don't have what you should have, even what you think you have will be taken away from you (Lk. 8:18).

Again, Jesus told of a nobleman who went into a far country after giving each of ten slaves 100 denarii. The story ends with an account of how severely the nobleman dealt with his slaves.

Have you ever wondered why Jesus' stories end with such stern warnings? They deal with issues of life and death. The Bible's central theme is the utter necessity of saving faith in Jesus Christ.

Christ's plan offers the sinner life through faith in Him. What follows? The saved sinner must tell other sinners how to find life in Christ.

Remember the occasion when Jesus pointed to the fields white with grain ready to be cut. He encouraged his disciples to bring in others from the human harvest saying,

*Already the reaper is getting paid and is gathering grain
for everlasting life (Jn. 4:36).*

The grain represented countless people Christ wanted His
followers to bring to Him.

What We Know Makes Us Responsible

Christ has told us His plan for the world. He summed up
in one sentence the wide task of His church. Notice carefully
Acts 1:8 and what follows:

*When He had said this, and while they were watching Him,
He was lifted up, and a cloud took Him away so they couldn't
see Him anymore. As He was going and they were gazing up
into the sky, two men in white clothes were standing right
beside them. "Men of Galilee," they asked "why are you
standing here looking up to heaven? This Jesus, who was
taken away from you to heaven, will come back the same
way you saw Him go to heaven" (Acts 1:9-11).*

Christ had just given His disciples a worldwide task. The
angels reminded them the work could not be done by gazing
skyward. Doing was demanded. Workers for the Lord were
needed.

Our assets add to our accountablility. "If you were given
much, much will be expected of you." You may remember
Christ told of *". . . a rich man who used to dress in purple
and fine linen and live in luxury every day"* (Luke 16:19).
That man landed in hell. We who hope for heaven by God's
unmerited grace must view life differently because we belong to Christ. Do the things we call ours really belong to us?

The Bible tells us the whole of our life is a stewardship.
We will be judged at the last by what we've done with the
things God trusted to us. Our Lord pictured it, saying:

It's like a man going on a trip. He called his slaves and put his money in their hands. He gave one man $10,000, another $4,000, and another $2,000, each according to his ability. Then he left (Matt. 25:14-15).

The two men who got the larger amounts invested them and each doubled his assets. But the one who got $2,000 went and dug a hole in the ground and hid his master's money. When the master returned the two men who did well were praised and given a larger commission. The man who failed was charged with being a "wicked and lazy slave," what was trusted to him was taken away and he heard the words,

Throw this good-for-nothing slave out into the dark where there will be crying and grinding of teeth (Matt. 25:30).

What We Do Makes A Difference

Applied to our own lives this is a sobering picture, is it not? Someone asks, "Is it fair? Why must we return our Master's assets with increase? Why must we invest to help finish world evangelization?" Because lives are at stake. The eternal well-being of numberless people is in the balance. Life and death are at issue.

Things you and I do make a difference, and so do things we fail to do. Our decisions affect the destinies of others. That fact was impressed on me by a letter from Roger Loa, a Chinese man I heard speak at Hinson Church in Portland, Oregon. Later he sent us a letter from his home in Taiwan which said in part:

For me this was without doubt the trip of a lifetime. I hope I'll be able to see you again, either in Taiwan, or the U.S.A. If not, however, I'll see you one day in heaven because you cared for my soul enough to send someone to tell me how to go there. Thank you one and all.

Roger Loa found eternal life because certain believers obeyed Christ's command to go with God's good news to earth's farthest parts. Are your efforts contributing to the salvation of souls out on Christianity's frontiers? Investment in that task will pay eternal dividends, because:

Christ Re-Aligns Our Purpose

Jesus told a man who had invited him to a meal:

When you give a dinner or a supper, don't invite your friends, your brothers, your relatives, or rich neighbors. Otherwise they'll invite you too and pay you back. No, when you give a banquet, invite the poor, crippled, lame, and blind. Then you'll be happy because they can't pay you back. You'll be paid back! when the righteous rise from the dead (Lk. 24:12-14).

Who are so *"poor"* and *"blind"* as those who have never heard the gospel? Think of the millions in people groups where no church exists. They could not be saved if they wanted to because no one has told them the way. The Church must never turn aside from the priority of the unfinished task. But can we seriously face that reality without coming closer to a wartime life style?

To really change our life style to simpler living is hard. It is not easy to give up luxuries to which we have become accustomed. We feel we deserve these good things and that God has filled our lives with abundance for our enjoyment.

Christ Asks Us to be Focused

But we can learn from men like Hudson Taylor, founder of the China Inland Mission. Taylor tells how he came to see that "all through the New Testament the coming of the Lord was the great hope of His people." He noted that though the time was not revealed the important thing was to be ready.

The believer should be prepared to give an account of his stewardship with joy and not with grief. As a result, Taylor looked through his little library and small wardrobe for things he would not want to give account for should Christ come at once. He gave books to poor neighbors and distributed clothing in other directions. After that he found it very helpful to him to go through his house from basement to attic from time to time with this object in view. It always caused him joy and blessing. Think what could be accomplished if Christians everywhere would channel unneeded resources into the Church's thrust toward unreached peoples. What a great way to increase our eagerness for Christ's coming!

But don't underestimate the challenge of a simple lifestyle focusing on the unfinished task. On every hand are Christians who know little of commitment. As our Lord indicated, the conflict can go either way. Some will prove they "can be trusted." They will focus on finishing the task and be found faithful when Christ comes. Some will settle for selfishness. How solemn in that context are Christ's words, *"...the master... will cut him in pieces and put him with the unfaithful"* (Lk. 12:46).

God requires an honest response. Remember,

You can't please God without faith. If you come to God, you must believe He exists and will always reward those who search for Him (Heb.11:6).

Our search for Him will cause us to identify with the work He has given us to do. The suddenness of His coming will permit no time for change, as when deadly volcanic gases one day erupted without warning from Mount Vesuvius. Those lethal gases immobilized people in a moment's time. Their forms are visible today in the ruins of Pompeii transfixed in the exact postures in which death suddenly took them. In Luke 12 the divine camera shows people in postures in which Christ will find them when He comes.

Christ Asks Us to be Faithful

To know and to do what He wants despite the indifference and apathy of others, pleases Him. The Apostle Paul wrote to the believers at Rome,

It's time now for you to wake up from sleep because we are now nearer being rescued than when we first believed (Rom. 13:11).

To be ready means to work, give, and pray for the completion of the world task. Readiness will require some to move to distant lands to pioneer for Christ.

Andrew Stirrett, a pharmacist in Canada, at age thirty-seven heard a sermon on the return of Christ. He said,

There came before me vividly my great sin of omission, my failure to tell those who know not the gospel. The question was insistent, "Will Jesus be pleased if He comes to find me behind the counter?" There was only one answer.

Stirrett sold his business, turned over his stores and four apartments to the young Sudan Interior Mission and started for Africa before they had considered his application. This quiet, gentle, goal oriented little man left on such short notice he didn't have time to say goodbye to his relatives. He crossed to England on a cattle boat to save money.

In Liverpool he enrolled in a course in tropical medicine while the puzzled mission wrestled with the problem of whether to accept him. When he finished his course and wrote from England saying he was ready to sail for Nigeria, the Council finally accepted him "on suspicion rather than on probation" as the founder later recalled.

Stirrett launched into the work at Patigi on the Niger River 500 miles into Nigeria's unreached interior. He never married and his severance with home ties was so complete that he had little thought for furloughs. Of his forty-six years with Sudan Interior Mission, forty-one were spent in Africa.

His passion was to take the gospel to people who did not know it. He thought of little else. In his words,

What a glorious privilege to go into one of these tribes and unlock to a whole nation the door of eternal life!

Dr. Stirrett used to say, *"I never had a call."* He was driven by the command of Scripture and his great concern for those who did not have the gospel. His appeal to young people was,

Come! The Lord is coming very soon, and you will surely have to meet Him. Do you want Him to find you in your easy chair" If He should come today, what would He find you doing?

God's kingdom continues to expand because obedient Christians pray, give and go. The gospel's power to bring lives under Christ's lordship prepares people for His return. As you stand on the foundation of God's revealed truth, what is your answer to Him? Remember, advance news of Christ's coming is better than gold. May it be so for you.

Chapter Seven

Rugged Reality

A chap flunked out of college and was too scared to go home and face his father. Instead he sent a telegram to his father's best friend which read, "Flunked out. Be home tomorrow. Prepare Dad."

Back came the answer, "Dad prepared. Prepare yourself!" Yes, we must face reality if we are to be ready for life's crises. A rugged world confronts us all around. It takes tough-mindedness to cope.

November 15, 1985, inhabitants of Armero, Colombia, heard a roar as a nearby ancient volcano blew up. Ulises Molano, a resident there, said,

When we heard the eruption, we left our home and went to the fire department, but they told us it was nothing and they were not going to sound the siren because it would frighten people.

The result? Over 23,000 people died that night, buried under an expanse of mud a mile wide. Reality was kept from them, so they died.

What meaning is there for us in the tragic mistake those men made? We must see humanity in the light of truth.

Hope For the Unreached Hinges on Us

The Bible reveals that people who have not received Christ are lost and hopeless. But God loves our race and "...*wants* all people to be saved and to come to know the truth" (1 Tim. 2:4). God's love is the foundation of our hope. The Apostle John wrote "We love because He first loved us" (1 Jn. 4:19). We answer God's love by giving our lives to Him. We do what He wants. Ask yourself how "tough love" should respond to the following passage. God's Word says:

Rescue those being led away to death; hold back those staggering towards slaughter. If you say, "But we knew nothing about this," does not He who weighs the heart perceive it? Does not He who guards your life know it? Will He not repay each person according to what He has done? (Prov. 24:11-12 NIV).

Those words are rugged, but true. Measure your life by them. Ask yourself, "Does what I do support what I believe?"

If the reality God's Word presents is alarming, then be alarmed! To be soothed when danger threatens may mean death. Those officials in Armero meant well. But their desire not to "frighten people" instead spelled their doom. We must avoid their mistake. In the real world of truth the Bible tells us that:

To Save People We Must Accept Reality

Our situation might be easier if truth were less stern. We may wonder why life for unreached peoples should depend on us. Or we may want to dodge responsibility as Cain tried to do when he asked, *"Am I my brother's keeper?"* But tough love requires us to recognize that the Bible is right.

God's world operation counts on every Christian to help *"rescue those being led away to death; hold back those staggering towards slaughter."* To that truth we must respond. Beware of false fantasies with which unbelief would blind us.

Someone once asked Abraham Lincoln, "If you call a horse's tail a leg, how many legs has the horse?" Said Lincoln, "Four! No matter what you call the tail it is still a tail." Likewise the Bible teaches us to call things truthfully by their right names. We must be moved by the fact that the unreached are far from God's fold. *"You too were dead in your transgressions and sins"* (Eph.2:1). That is the condition of all who have not heard God's good news and trusted Christ. That need brought God's Son from heaven to die. If spiritual life could have been found apart from Christ He would not have said, *"I came so that they will have life..." (Jn. 10:10).*

Have you thought why the Bible asks us to *"rescue the captives from death"?* We accept reality by agreeing that people groups beyond gospel frontiers are *"dead in trespasses and sins."*

God Says They Are Lost and Dead

We can all visualize how threatening physical death is. My wife and I remember a winter morning in Nyack, New York. We answered a knock at our door and were told a wealthy neighbor, clad in a bloodstained bathrobe, was begging a ride to a hospital. He had been shot seven times by his butler. His blood stained my car seat as I rushed him to the operating room where doctors struggled to save his life. Amazingly he lived and later sent me a letter thanking me, as he said, "for the icy and bloodsoaked ride which saved my life. He knew he had barely missed death. But those unreached with the gospel do not know they face eternal death. We sense Jesus' love for them when He says, *"I have other sheep too, that are not in this fold. I must lead those too."*(Jn. 10:16), but they are barred from salvation by not knowing where or how to find the shepherd.

Newspapers reported the finding of a woman's body on the hot sands of California's Mojave Desert. She was gathering material for a feature story and lost her way in the desert. In her search for water, she came upon a cabin and broke a window to enter. She found no water but left $3.00 with the following note, "I am exhausted and must have water. I do not think I can last much longer." The cabin owner found the note and began to search for the woman. Her body was found only two miles from a spring with abundant water. She died because she did not know where the water was.

We know the One who gives *"living water. . bubbling with everlasting life"* (Jn. 4:10,14). He has ordered us to ". . . preach the good news to the whole world" (Mk. 16:15). We own Him as our Lord. One conclusion follows: God wants us to bring in the unreached. We must tell them who Christ is because they do not know. How strongly the Apostle Paul argues,

But how can they call on Him if they haven't believed in Him? How can they believe in Him, if they haven't heard of Him? How can they hear if nobody preaches? (Rom. 10:14).

God Asks Us to Go Where They Are

Only "reaching the unreached" expand God's kingdom. That is why it was Paul's practice to go with the *"...good news only where Christ's name wasn't known ..." (Rom. 15:20).* God gave Paul the method that should have become basic practice for every church during the present age. It is God's way to insure nonstop progress. Outreach is assured so long as we practice Paul's procedure. Christianity will continue to fill the earth so long as our prime focus is to *"tell the good news only where Christ's name is not known."*

The importance of applying this truth today can hardly be exaggerated. Where churches are in decline, this is the task that will turn them around. This is the secret of success, the thrust we dare not dilute. People groups that lie beyond present gospel frontiers are the target we must keep in our sights.

God loves all the peoples of the world. He asks us to focus on pioneer outreach in order to offer the greatest good to the greatest number of lost people. They are dead to God and face a hopeless future. When the Church forgets that, the results are tragic. When we obey and go, results are glorious.

Our service will be flawed if we fail to accept the reality that people unreached with the gospel are truly lost. The Bible says, *"All who sin without having the law will perish without the law"* (Rom. 2:12). God's Word pictures the plight of those without the gospel as sad beyond words. They live in night, they die without hope, they face darkness forever. That truth should ring like an alarm gong in the bell tower of our hearts.

Since hope for unreached people hinges on our obedience,

To Save People We Must
Actively Respond

The Bible warns us to avoid the trap of saying, "Look, this isn't our business." We dare not hide behind the excuse that we didn't know the unreached were lost. Far better to trust the Bible and obey God's marching orders. There is a message of hope for the world's people. There is good news by which they can be saved eternally. We must pay the price to carry God's message to them all.

Obstacles are sure to confront obedient Christians, but they can be overcome. Remember how early believers were arrested and imprisoned as they shared God's good news. The officials warned them never again to speak to anyone in Jesus' name.

Peter and John answered them, "Does God consider it right to listen to you and not to God? Judge for yourselves. We cannot stop telling what we have seen and heard" (Acts 4:19-20).

One such obstacle to finding enough workers for God's harvest can be the influence of parents. Many withhold their children from service for Christ abroad. The whole progress of God's redemptive plan is impacted by such disobedience. The example of parents is powerful. Mr. and Mrs. Gratton Guinness heard J. Hudson Taylor and were convinced they should leave England to serve Christ in some unreached area. Instead they were asked to take charge of a Training College in a poor section of East London to prepare others to go. They talked to their children from infancy about the Lord and each trusted Christ personally by age four.

Their son, Whitfield, at fourteen, was baptized and joined the church with the goal of going where the gospel had not yet been preached. From his parents and the trainees, he sensed constant concern to honor God's priority. Whitfield got his medical degree and was ready to go to China. But his family was now scattered leaving only his mother at home. He asked her, "How can I also go far away and leave you alone?" She replied,

My son, do you so little know your mother? Do you not realize that it is my ambition, my heart's desire, to see you all - every one of my children – serving the Lord where the need is greatest? I would not keep you back one hour!

Under the China Inland Missiori, Whitfeild went to the province of Honan, China, where more than 35 million people existed with no witness for Christ. There he labored for Christ twenty-seven years until his death.

It Will Cost Full Surrender

Before me is a letter telling of Rick, whose mother led him to Christ in a North African country where the law forbids any open witness for Christ. Not long ago in a coffee shop, he explained the gospel to a cousin and another friend. The next day, three policemen took Rick to the police station and questioned him for four hours before letting him go. Shortly thereafter, Rick was traveling on a bus with another cousin to whom he gave his testimony. Apparently his words were overheard. A secret policeman a few seats in front of them confronted Rick and ordered him to take the next bus back to where he had come from. Despite these problems, Rick is unashamed to be counted among the redeemed. God has His own who are truly lights in dark places. We must support their testimony.

God asks your all. Paul pled with the Christians at Rome,

... give your bodies as a living sacrifice .. let yourselves be transformed by the renewing of your minds... (Rom. 12:1-2).

He called the Corinthians to yield fully to Christ saying,

He died for all that those who live should no longer live for themselves but for Him who died and rose for them (II Cor. 5:15).

Christ's love will powerfully enable you. Jesus said, *"Anything can be done if you believe"* (Mk. 9:23).

Audubon, the great birdwatcher and painter, did some amazing things. He was driven by a passion to understand the life of the birds of North America and to portray them in their natural surroundings. It is said he would often wade into a swamp until only his head remained above water There he would stand for hours as poisonous snakes swam by and other dangers threatened. Why did he do it? Simply to be able to paint one more bird in its habitat. Audubon fulfilled his ambition to do what others had not done. So it is that even young people with scant experience do exploits. Recently President Reagan honored four young Americans including Trevor Ferrell, 13, of Philadelphia. Two years ago, Trevor began taking blankets and food to homeless people. He had seen their plight dramatized on television. There are now 250 volunteers in "Trevor's Campaign for the Homeless." They feed up to 200 people a night. Reagan said afterward, "Nothing is impossible; no victories beyond our reach."

You may say, "But what can I do? I'm just a common Christian." Whoever you are, God knows you and has a place for you in His rescue force. During my travels in the Indian subcontinent I was deeply impressed with young people who have gone there with the gospel. They are genuinely effective for Christ. Why? It is not that they are more talented than others. But they have proved they are available to God by going. That makes the difference.

Such availability reminds me of a letter that I prize from a young couple who went recently to a so-called "closed land" as members of a Christian team. The letter ends with these words:

You are a special part of this team. The people here know so little about the Lord that even with our limited language we can still communicate our hope. This is what makes life here so exciting. If you care to join us over here, they sure need your witness.

Another avenue for expanding truly pioneer missions projects is to give wisely to those who are doing the job. "Back to the Bible Broadcast" of Lincoln, Nebraska, has reaped a harvest of souls in India. There, they broadcast the gospel daily to an area where 300 million Hindi-speaking people live. Many thousands have been saved. They also sponsor gospel projects abroad through other agencies. In any such case, they require that every dollar received go to the designated project without deduction. Such work is worthy of support.

It Will Claim First Place

Our text reminds us that each must answer to God for the use of time, talents and assets. An hour of reckoning is ahead. Each will *". . receive according to what he has done with his life"* (II Cor. 5:10).

As we make our choices we should always be aware *that ". . . each of us will have to give an account of himself to God"* (Rom. 14:12). It should be our primary concern to focus on peoples who are God's priority to take the gospel beyond its current frontiers That is the way to finish the task.

But remember, a priority makes demands. I learned that in Argentina one day while working on a pump motor at the bottom of a twenty-foot well. Our son, Tim, about ten years old, started down the well to bring me a tool, and slipped. I heard his cry, thrust out both arms and caught him as he fell backwards. The jolt almost knocked me flat but probably saved Tim from breaking his back on the motor. The moment I heard his cry, Tim's safety became my priority, the one thing that mattered. Unless we really focus on unreached peoples, other needs close at hand will fill our lives.

In New Orleans, I spoke to a businessmen's group about the desperate plight of unreached people. At the close the chairman prayed, "Oh God, you know that New Orleans is just as dark as darkest Africa." I felt like saying, "Who are you kidding?" People in New Orleans have access to saving truth in many ways. Anyone can hear the gospel by radio or TV, get a Bible, find a church, read Christian literature or talk with a believer. In countless areas in Africa there are no such avenues to Christ.

How recently have you asked yourself "What am I really living for?" I recall an experience that helped me with that question. I was flying from Costa Rica to New Orleans. A businessman boarded the plane in Honduras and sat beside me. He was a lumberman who for years had operated a mill in Louisiana. As timber was used up, he moved his mill to another part of the state. Timber got scarce there also. He heard there was lumber in Honduras, went there and built a mill. When I met him, he had been traveling back and forth for several years, his family in Louisiana, his work in Honduras. I thought, "What a life of sacrifice!" But the man said no such thing. His goal was to make money. He lived for that.

God's priority for us is to offer eternal life to everyone. The organization I work with focuses on Islam. Fifteen percent of the world's people are Muslims. You might assume we would be sending them that proportion of the 50,000 witnesses for Christ who go abroad from the United States. Instead, we have been sending them less than one percent.

Today we sense in many lives a fresh vision. More young people are owning God's priority: finish the world task. Recently several couples went with that aim to a North African country. One night three of the families were arrested and jailed. After a few hours the police released the women and children. The three men were held thirty days in a pest-ridden jail. The families were then deported from the country without a trial. They are now in the process of regrouping, seeking another needy field. Tough love does not flinch in the face of hardships. Hope for unreached peoples hinges on obedience to Christ.

Chapter Eight

Commitment Counts

Someone said to James Farmer, former Director of the Commission on Racial Equality, "What do you want from me? I'm just an innocent bystander."

Farmer answered, "If you're a bystander, you're not innocent." Guilt felt by "spectator Christians" is often revealed by a defensive attitude. The best way to rid oneself of such guilt is by getting involved in Christ's work. His, *"Follow Me,"* is a divine call to active engagement in world evangelization. Focus today is on finishing the world task. Christ pointed out the inadequacy of routine religion when he said,

These people honor Me with their lips, but their hearts are far away from Me. They worship Me in vain (Matt. 15:8).

Pleasing Him is the focus of this chapter. The Apostle Paul expressed his longing with the words, *"Now whether we live here or move out, we try hard to please Him" (II Cor. 5:9). To others he wrote, "You learned from us how you must live and please God"(I Thess.4:1).*

Love for Christ Is Compelling

A believer's desire to please Christ lights up the following narrative:

While Jesus was in Bethany in the home of Simon the leper and was lying at the table, a woman came with an alabaster

jar of perfume, real nard and very expensive. She broke the jar and poured the perfume on His head. Some who were there felt annoyed and said to one another, "Why was the perfume wasted like this? This perfume could have been sold for more than three hundred denarii and the money given to the poor." And they were grumbling at her. "Let her alone," Jesus said. "Why should you trouble her? She has done a beautiful thing to Me. The poor you always have with you, and you can help them whenever you want to, but you will not always have Me. She has done what she could. She came ahead of time to pour the perfume on My body to prepare it for burial. I tell you wherever the good news is preached in the whole world, certainly what she has done will also be told in memory of her" (Mk.14:3-9).

The account is intriguing. We note Christ's eloquent tribute to Mary as He said, *"She has done what she could."* He made her a great promise, saying,

Wherever the good news is preached in the whole world, certainly what she has done will also be told in memory of her.

A remarkable prophecy! The quality of Mary's love for Christ is this story's hallmark. Originally, a hallmark was an official stamp on gold and silver articles indicating a standard of purity. It was a proof of genuineness or good quality. Our Lord marks love that is genuine. On the eve of His crucifixion Jesus said to his disciples, *"If you love Me, you will do what I order"* (Jn. 14:15). *Again, 'If you have My commandments and obey them, you love Me"* (Jn. 14:21). After His resurrection the same thought surfaces. Three times in succession He asked Peter, *"Do you love Me?"* (Jn. 21:15-17). What would you answer if He asked you that?

The strength of our love for Jesus distinguishes our faith from mere "Christian religion." Mary was powerfully moved as she came with the alabaster jar of perfume, "... broke the jar and poured the perfume on His head (Mk. 14:3). Who was this One who so profoundly influenced Mary? The Old Testament prophesies His coming and profiles His person. Book by book the portrait becomes more clear.

David wrote of Him saying,

The Lord says to my Lord, "Sit at My right till I make Your enemies Your footstool" (Ps. 110:1).

When we reach Isaiah, written eight hundred years before Christ, the picture has added detail. To him God says,

Here is My Servant whom I support; I have chosen Him, and I delight in Him. I put My Spirit on Him. He will bring righteousness to the nations (Isa. 42:1).

Psalmists and prophets were captivated by Christ's person long before He came. Millions since then have demonstrated that:

Loving Christ Creates a Relationship

To follow Christ is not like keeping a code of conduct. Self-discipline can produce a certain level of performance. As time passes, it tends to become rigid and traditional. Dedication to following Christ is quite different. The act of becoming a Christian produces a personal relationship. Christ invites us to this relationship with Himself. How comforting are His words,

Come to Me, all you who are working hard and carrying a heavy load, and I will give you rest. Take My yoke on you, and learn from Me; I am gentle and humble-minded; then you will find your rest (Matt.11:28-29).

The Apostle Paul illustrates the Intimacy of the relation between the believer and his Lord. Paul was no ordinary man. His strength of mind was magnificent. He could soar like an eagle to explore the heights of heavenly truth or descend to plumb the depths of the divine purpose. But when Paul wanted to share the very heart of his faith in Christ he said simply, Christ *"...loved me and gave Himself for me"* (Gal. 2:20). There is light and music and sweetness in those words. They are like all the bright spring mornings in one glorious dawning, or all the songs ever sung in one anthem. They are like all the flowers that ever bloomed in one bouquet: *"He loved me and gave Himself for me."* Elsewhere Paul returned to the theme saying:

But any advantages I had I considered a loss for Christ. Yes, I think it is all a loss because it is so much better to know Christ Jesus, my Lord. For Him I have lost everything and consider it garbage in order to win Christ and find myself in Him, not having my own righteousness based on the Law but the righteousness that depends on faith, that God gives those who believe in Christ (Phil.3:7-9).

Love Followed His Lead

Mary could have held her giving to the level of those around her. Many do that. Instead, she gave a gift of perfume worth more than 300 denarii. A denarius was a day's wage for a working man. So Mary's gift was worth 300 days' work. Have you ever given ten months' wages in one gift to Jesus Christ? I hope you have. When we ask ourselves why half the world's people have not yet heard God's good news one reason we must consider is shallow giving. Mary supported his purpose in her day. Christ explained Mary's act, saying, *"She came ahead of time to pour the perfume on My body to prepare it for burial."* Mary, living in the time before Christ's death, helped prepare Him for the cross. Christ clearly taught that He was about to die; that was His aim.

The Son of Man has to suffer much, be rejected by the elders, the ruling priests, and the Bible scholars, be killed, and then rise on the third day (Mk. 8:31). The Son of Man is going to be betrayed into the hands of men and they will kill Him, but on the third day; after He's killed, He will rise (Mk. 9:31). Look, we're going up to Jerusalem and the Son of Man will be betrayed to the ruling priests and the Bible scholars, who will condemn Him to die and hand Him over to the Gentiles. They'll mock Him and spit on Him, scourge Him and kill Him. But on the third day He will rise (Mk. 10:33).

Mary shared in accomplishing Christ's prime purpose then.

To follow Christ we must find where he is now.

Love Follows Where He Leads Today

We who look back on the cross have the privilege of identifying with His present purpose. Before His death Christ stated His aim for our age, saying, *"I tell you wherever the good news is preached in the whole world."* It is this plain, often-repeated purpose which many believers today have somehow missed.

To follow the living Christ is exciting. Spontaneous desire to please Him results from being born again. The hub of life shifts from self to Christ. As a university student, I came to know Him. My habit of swearing disappeared. I remember no effort to curb it. Plainly, profanity would not please Him. That was enough. Other bad habits may be harder to get rid of. The perfume Mary brought was *"very expensive."*

So too, the Christian may find it costly to please Jesus Christ, He wants us to be great givers as indicated by His words, *"Give these things as you received them – without pay"* (Matt.10:8).

Yet some care deeply about Christ's cause. I think of the wife of George C. Weiss of Back to the Bible Broadcast. Olga was an earnest Christian. She had a weak heart caused perhaps by rheumatic fever when she was small. Their doctor one day told George, "One of the hardest things for her is to carry the wet wash out of the basement and hang those clothes on the line. If it is at all possible, she should have a clothes dryer. It will add years to her life." Though dryers were costly at that time, George bought one for his wife. He hid it in the garage and on Christmas eve took Olga and showed it to her. A few days later, before it had been installed, she heard her husband's appeal on the broadcast for a need in India. She phoned him at the office and asked, "Do you think we could sell the dryer and give the money for India?"

Struggling to control his voice, George said, "Let's talk about that later." That evening he told her, "Let's leave it this way. If the Lord sends in the amount of money we are asking for, then let that be a sign He wants you to keep the dryer. But if enough doesn't come in, we'll sell it." They were able to keep the dryer, but not because she was thinking of herself. She longed to please the Lord by getting the gospel to everyone everywhere. Love for Christ is strong.

To become a Christian relates one intimately to Christ's person. To be linked to His person means involvement with His purpose. Some years ago an evangelical publication printed several messages of mine. Later, I was invited to speak to the staff. On a second visit, I challenged them to consider serving overseas in places of deeper spiritual darkness. The editor wrote me disapproving my asking his people to think about giving themselves to meet needs abroad. But though some Christians may not favor taking the good news overseas, God wants it done. Jesus said,

You ". . . will testify of Me to . . the farthest parts of the world" (Acts 1:8). He also said, "...where I am, there My servant will be"(Jn. 12:26). Love for Christ is strong. In every generation faithful followers have been willing to go with Christ to the ends of the earth.

Love for Christ Accepts His Priorities

The prominence of Christ's Great Commission in the New Testament proves His purpose to see the world evangelized with God's good news. Those who love Him share that purpose. A young woman from an American home obeyed Christ's command to preach the gospel to every creature. She said good-bye to friends, culture and comforts, went to India then north to the very Tibetan border. Everywhere, she ministered to lepers. One day she noticed something strange about her hand. She looked at it carefully and saw that it was leprous. Going into her room she shut the door. Spreading out her hand before God she said,

Father, here is my hand. I am a leper. I am willing to die. I would like to live if I could live for these people. If you will touch and heal me, I will give the balance of my life to lepers.

That prayer was heard. The hand that healed lepers long ago touched her hand and the leprosy vanished. For thirty years, Mary Reed labored for Christ among the lepers in that lonely land. No one could doubt her personal devotion to the Son of God. She made Christ's purpose her own. True love for Christ is strong.

His Cause Claims All

Love is practical, wanting what He wants. Jesus said, *"She has done what she could."* The grumbling disapproval of those around Mary could not thwart her purpose. She was moved by a superior force As Paul put it, *"The love of Christ compels us."*

Melville Cox was the first Methodist missionary to Liberia, Africa. He went in 1833 when West Africa was known as "the white man's grave." Cox was severely criticized when he announced his purpose to go there with the gospel. He was told that he was flying in the face of providence and that no white man could live in Liberia. Cox listened, prayed, and held to his purpose. At Wesleyan University in Boston one of the students taunted him saying, "Better take your coffin with you."

Cox answered, "If I die in Africa, come out and write my epitaph."

The student asked, "What shall I write?"

Said Cox, "Write, let a thousand fall before Africa be given up." Across every later generation that answer has rebuked unbelief.

Melville Cox died less than five months after reaching Liberia. Like his Master he was only thirty-three years old when he went into eternity. Yet, how eagerly he went abroad and how hard he worked compelled by Christ's love. His affirmations live on:

Let a thousand fall before Africa be given up.

I am not afraid to die.

Never give up the mission.

What is dark to me is light to Him.

Africa must be redeemed though thousands fall.

I want to know all that a man can know of God and live.

Love releases one from lesser claims, to live and obey Christ. It frees the individual front bondage to peoples' opinions. Mary's companions complained that the *"perfume could have been sold for more than 300 denarii and the money given to the poor."* Mary had a higher purpose.

Only a few years later, Peter and John surprised the leaders of their day who were trying to silence their witness for Christ. When their adversaries found out that they had *".. no education or training, they were surprised to see how boldly they spoke. Then they realized these men had been with Jesus"* (Acts 4:13).

Other Causes Must Yield

When my wife and I applied to serve in West China and Tibet with the Christian Missionary Alliance, we were hindered by friends. They tried hard to persuade us we were mistaken. They told us how much we were needed in the United States, what good work we were doing, how others could go abroad, etc. Pre-Pearl Harbor tensions increased and our passports were cancelled. Four years later, we were appointed to go to Argentina. To our surprise the same kind of opposition surfaced. We were puzzled to learn that Christians were not in favor of our going. Since then we have discovered how common that attitude is.

The Apostle Paul faced similar opposition. Remember how God stopped him on the Damascus road and flooded his life with light. From that hour, Paul had a one-track mind. He kept moving out. Let's call him to the witness stand and ask, "Paul, how did you show your love for Christ?"

Paul answers, *"... I didn`t disobey what I saw from heaven"* (Acts 26:19).

We can imagine the voices of his friends, "Paul, don't go to Rome. There's plentv of need right here in Jerusalem."

He replies, *"I must help Greeks and non-Greeks, the wise and the foolish"* (Rom 1:14)

"Paul, don't be a fanatic. Stay In Judea."

He says,

I was ambitious to tell the good news only where Christ's name wasn't known, so as not to build on any foundation others had laid, but as it is written: "Those who were never told about Him will see, and those who never heard will understand" (Rom 15:20-21).

Another says, "Paul, be reasonable. You'll get yourself killed."

Paul answers,

I don't count my life worth anything. I just want to finish running my race and doing the work the Lord Jesus entrusted to me, declaring the good news of God's love (Acts 20:24).

On and on Paul goes. Criticisms can't cool his zeal, punishments can't change his purpose, stonings can't stop him. Nor could jails, perils, persecutions, or anything men or demons could hurl at him. Through it all Paul persevered until he could say,

It's time for me to leave. I fought the good fight, I ran the race, I kept the faith (II Tim. 4:6).

There is always an open door for the person committed to obeying Christ. Only 600 of the 14,000 towns in Spain have an evangelical church. Barcelona has a strong Christian witness. A telephone company employee there knew his witness for Christ would count more in a place where spiritual darkness was deeper. He sought a transfer and was sent to Caceres, a town 160 miles southwest of Madrid. We visited his home there, the hub of a new testimony for Christ. Should that case be uncommon? Thousands of Christians could move to places where Christ is not known. Why not, if love for Christ is strong?

Love acts promptly. Mary did not hesitate. When she broke the alabaster box and poured the perfume on Christ's head it was probably her last chance. The cross was close. Christ was about to be betrayed. The very next verse tells of Judas' treachery. What if Mary had been frightened off by the frowns of the critics? What if she had surrendered to the cold and hostile stares? What if she had delayed giving her gift? Then the deed would never have been done. The perfume would never have been poured on Christ's head. His words of commendation would never have been spoken. The story of her love would never have circled the world. So much depended on her acting right then. Jesus put it well, *"She did what she could!"*

To us she says, "Don't wait to do for Christ what is in your heart. Act while you can. It may be later than you think. Future regrets won't make up for today's failure. Do now what you ought to do. Soon you will stand in your Lord's presence. Whatever you give now will seem too little then. So do all you can. Love for Christ, responding to His love for us, is strong."

I will place no value
on anything I have or may posess
except in relation
to the kingdom of Christ.

If anything will advance
the interests of that kingdom,

it shall be given or kept
only as by giving or keeping it
I may advance the glory of Him
to whom I owe all my hopes

for time
and for eternity.

-David Livingstone

Jesus said,

"Seek ye first the kingdom of God
and His righteousness."

-Mt.6:33 KJV

Chapter Nine

God's Coming Kingdom

Years ago, I climbed a high hill on the north side of the Missouri River near Sioux City, Iowa. My goal was to reach an impressive stone shaft erected by Iowa Presbyterians. When I stood breathless by the stone, three names could be seen carved there, with the words:

In memory of pioneer missionaries who on April 29, 1869, from this hilltop viewed the great unchurched areas, and after prayer went out to win the west for Christ.

I thanked God that day for people in every age whose hearts have belonged to Him for His work. They determined to be a part of what God was doing in the world, Such people paid the price to put God's kingdom first in their lives. In this chapter we will see how we can accelerate the coming of God's kingdom. To live with that aim gives life meaning.

"God's kingdom" is a theme that spans the whole Bible. In Genesis we find Jacob's prophecy,

The scepter will not pass away from Judah until Shiloh [Man of Rest] comes, whom the nations will obey (Gen. 49:10).

To King David God promised a Descendant, saying,

I will have Him stand in My house and in My kingdom forever, and His throne will be established forever (I Chr.17:14).

The prophet Daniel adds to the fascinating trail by explaining to King Nebuchadnezzar "what will happen in the future." He describes a day when:

. . the God of heaven will set up a kingdom that will never be destroyed; no other people will ever be permitted to rule over it; it will smash and bring to an end all these kingdoms and will stand forever (Dan.2:44).

Thus God's coming kingdom spans the Old Testament.

When John the Baptist appeared he cried, *"Repent, the kingdom of heaven is here" (Mt. 3:1).* Soon Jesus began to preach, *"Repent, the kingdom of heaven is here!"* (Mt. 4:17). He taught his followers to pray, "Your kingdom come." The Apostles spoke of God's present and future kingdom. Paul constantly emphasized it. The last verse of Acts records how he *"preached God's kingdom."* This theme continues to its crescendo in the Book of Revelation when loud voices in heaven cry,

The kingdom of the world has become the kingdom of our Lord and of His Christ and He will be king forever (Rev. 11:15).

Thus we trace God's movement through history as we hear kings, prophets and apostles speak of His kingdom. That theme, rooted in the past, inspires us today by its promise of a glorious future. It embraces all our tomorrows. The Holy Spirit whispers:

"Work for God's Kingdom! It's Wise."

When our Lord taught His followers to pray, "Your kingdom come," He was setting the direction of their lives and ours. To identify daily with God's purpose for our world will affect what we do. Have you realized that t,o pray daily, *"Your will be done,"* is to respond to God's invitation to let Him take charge of your life? He may set your private plans aside. Dare you trust God that much?

Someone asked Emily Post, the noted authority on manners, what to do if an invitation to the White House were received which conflicted with a previous engagement. She answered, "An invitation to the White House is a summons which takes precedence over any previous engagement." We have God's written invitation to join those who are implementing His world redemptive plan. For us to set aside all other projects is profoundly wise. It is vital to understand that we are to:

"Live for God's Kingdom! It Honors Christ."

Once when Jesus was asked about His coming rule He answered, *"...the kingdom of God is within you"* (Lk.17:21 KJV). He wants your life to become God's kingdom in miniature. How? Ask God's Son each morning to occupy the throne of your heart. Your own life is the area you most completely control. Tell Him plainly that you put your whole being under his authority. Fully honor within yourself the lordship of Christ. Notice also that Jesus worked bodily at His God-given task. In Nazareth, where Jesus had been raised, He announced His mission. He did so by reading from the scroll of the prophet Isaiah where it says:

The Spirit of the Lord is on Me because He anointed Me to tell the poor the good news. He sent Me to announce to prisoners, "You are free," to the blind, "You will see again," to free those who are broken down, to announce a season when the Lord welcomes people (Lk. 4:18-19).

Those words describe the work Christ did on earth. Day after day his labors advanced God's eternal plan. In the same way we, His second body, must finish the task He began. To do that suggests that each of us reevaluate our reason for living. Seek seriously the meaning of Paul's strange words:

The love of Christ compels us because we're convinced One died for all and so all have died. He died for all that those who live should no longer live for themselves but for Him who died and rose for them (II Cor. 5:14-15).

Let Him Control You

Christians today seem strangely removed from the way of life those words indicate. David Shenk tells how a Muslim asked him, "Why don't Christians follow the way of Jesus?" Shenk was dining with his close friend in Washington, D.C., when the man leaned close and asked that disturbing question. He went on thoughtfully, "When I read the gospel I am overjoyed. The life and teachings of Jesus are wonderful, wonderful, really, truly wonderful. But please show me Christians who are willing to follow the way of Jesus." They sipped their spiced tea silently for a few moments, then he added, "I have met a few, very few people who try to follow Jesus. But they follow Him only in their private lives. Consequently, your American society has become very evil. It seems to me that 'you Christians' do not believe that the way of Jesus is practical. That makes me very sad."

The world task Christ gave His people is not hard to understand. Unbelief is our biggest obstacle. If we believe the Bible is true, we had better obey it. If not, as the Bible says, *"Let us eat, drink, and be merry for tomorrow we die."*

Let Him Command You

Samuel Zwemer was one who believed Christians must finish the task Christ began. During his senior year in college, a pioneer of the Student Volunteer Movement spoke on campus. He displayed a map of India with a metronome in front of it. He explained that each time it ticked one person in that subcontinent died who had never heard of Jesus Christ.

This so moved Zwemer that at the close of the meeting he signed the decision card, stating, "God helping me, I purpose to be a foreign missionary."

In seminary, with fellow student James Cantine, the two men chose Arabia, Islam's homeland, as the hardest field they could find. Later, turned down by mission boards as foolhardy for selecting so fanatical a target people, the men formed a new agency, the Arabian Mission.

Zwemer went to Arabia in 1890 and by 1905 had worked in Bahrain, Egypt, Iran, Iraq, Lebanon, and Saudi Arabia, selling Bibles, winning Muslims to Christ, and writing the first of more than fifty books on Islam. He had also married Amy Wilkes and together they had buried their first two daughters, smitten with dysentery, in Bahrain. Zwemer's later influence in student conferences was perhaps without parallel. Dr. Robert E. Speer, who knew him well, wrote,

Dr. Zwemer hung a great map of Islam before us and, with a sweep of his hand across all those darkened areas, said:

Thou O Christ art all I want and Thou O Christ art all they want. What Christ can do for any man, He can do for every man.

Zwemer and Speer perhaps caused more young people to choose to serve Christ in far fields than any other two men in history.

The Holy Spirit will work in a similar way in yielded lives today. Tough love will keep us from flinching when hard choices are demanded. Our Lord never promised us an easy path. To work for Christ's coming kingdom is wise. Simply recognize that each one of us must:

"Change for God's Kingdom! It's Worthwhile"

With good reason the Apostle Paul pleads with Christians to commit themselves fully to Christ. He writes:

I appeal to you, fellow Christians, by the mercies of God, to give your bodies as a living sacrifice, holy and pleasing to God, and so worship Him as thinking beings. Don't live like this world, but let yourselves be transformed by a renewing of your minds so you can test and be sure what God wants, what is good and pleasing and perfect (Rom. 12:1-2).

One alternative to the commitment to God demanded by this passage is its secular counterpart. There the objective is usually some mix of power, wealth, or fame. All are measures of success in the kingdom of this world.

Noted author and pastor, Chuck Swindoll, cites this poignant illustration:

Dennis Barnhart was president of an aggressive, rapidly growing company, Eagle Computer Incorporated. His life is a study in tragedy. From a small beginning, his firm grew incredibly fast. He finally decided they should go public. The forty-four year old man, as a result of his first public stock offering, became a multimillionaire virtually overnight. Then, for some strange reason, while he was in his red Ferrari only blocks from the company headquarters, he drove his car through twenty feet of guard rail into a ravine and died.

The Los Angeles Times reported the following:

"Until the accident at 4:30 Wednesday afternoon, it had been the best of days for Barnhart and the thriving young company which makes small business and Personal computers. Eagle netted $37 million from the initial offering of 2.75 million shares. The stock which hit the market at $13 a share quickly rose as high as $27 before closing at a bid price of $15.50. That made Barnhart's ownership of 592,000 shares worth more than $9 million."

That afternoon he died.

What of your kingdom? What of your plans for the future? What are you hanging onto? Dreams, of course. That's what keeps you going, right? Hope. Exciting plans. You're working on them now. You work on them on your vacation. And you think about them in your spare time. But you know, all of that seems terribly irrelevant when you face the fact that you'll be reduced to death in only a brief span of time. For some it could be less than a decade, for others, less than a year. For Barnhart, it was that same afternoon.

Let Him Change You

Always be available to Christ. Are you? An added dimension of strength operates in the yielded life. As the prophet Hanani said centuries ago,

The Lord's eyes scan the whole world to use His Strength for those whose hearts are altogether loyal to Him (II Chr. 16:9).

To have such a loyal heart we must begin with some essentials:

First, pray to the triune God as you start your day. Lift your heart to the Father, the Creator and Sustainer of all that is. Talk to Him, the Everlasting One, from eternity to eternity He is God. He is changeless, perfect in holiness, hating sin, loving righteousness, and dwelling in a light no mortal can approach. Still, His name is love, and He has come to us in the person of His Son.

Tell Jesus Christ you give Him the throne of your heart for the day. Say it with words. You may have done it before, perhaps only yesterday, but reaffirm it. Open every aspect of your life to Him. Don't keep any part off limits. Visualize your life as totally His kingdom for that day. Ask Him to use it somehow to accelerate the coming of His universal kingdom.

Pray to the Holy Spirit who lives in you that he will make it happen. He is your Comforter, Counselor, Teacher, and Guide. Ask him to take the things of Christ and make them real to you today, to make you sensitive to truth as you read His Word and as you relate to people. Remember, He is the *"Guarantee of our inheritance. "* Thank Him for transforming you by the renewing of your mind so you can experience the *"good, acceptable and perfect will of God"* (Rom. 12:2 KJV).

As you close your time with Him, remind God that you pray in the name of Jesus, who died for you and whose rising proved you justified, the One in whose wounds you hide. You plead the merit of Him who was exalted on high and given the name above every name. He is now at the right hand of God where He prays for you and from whence He is coming to receive you and to usher in His kingdom. Pray that prayer in substance to start each day. To work for Christ's coming kingdom is wise.

Second: get free from debt. In our land debt has become a huge problem. It seems so harmless and offers immediate benefits. With debt you can enjoy at once the things you want. Don't be deceived! Debt is a Trojan horse with power to destroy you. At best it is a ball and chain keeping countless Christians from serving God effectively. See it as an enemy; shun its snare. Debt is too large a subject to treat here in detail, but know its treacherous nature. It can destroy Christ's lordship in your life.

Third: choose world evangelism activities that accelerate closure of the gap between reached and unreached. Use God's coming kingdom as a touchstone to test things you might get involved in. Which of them exert influence to hasten Christ's return to establish His kingdom? Testing your options may change your priorities. Focus on gospel fronts worldwide. Learn about one or two people groups who have no church. Find out what efforts are being made to reach them. The goal is to see Christ become the hope of peoples living beyond present Christian boundaries. The world must be evangelized. That is the most important enterprise on earth.

Let Him Challenge You

This huge task requires help in many lands at many levels from many people. Your contribution may seem small, but your little when added to the efforts of many others becomes much. The raindrop is tiny, but enough of them water the earth. Knowing you are a part of a worldwide movement with a divine purpose gives inner strength. To live frugally as an end in itself means little. But to choose a simpler lifestyle in order to channel more support to church planters makes sense.

Live the communist slogan, "Everything for the front." God saved you to serve in His world rescue operation. Earlier I told how my conversion made the Bible intensely interesting to me. I discovered God wanted each believer to be part of His solution for the world's pain. I read, *"How beautiful is the coming of those who bring good news"* (Rom. 10:15). Those words well describe pioneering to plant churches.

Cameron Townsend of Wycliffe Bible Translators believed the primary goal of every translator was evangelization.

The overpowering motivation for this thrust was that if Christ had not already returned when every tribe and nation had been evangelized, He would then return. For this reason, Romans 15:20 became a central key to his mission - almost a rallying cry: *"I was ambitious to tell the good news only where Christ's name wasn't known."*

Esther Matteson, co-translator of the Piro New Testament, once asked Townsend to assign two more people to the Piros in order to train their young people for the ministry.

The request seemed legitimate. But Townsend longed to hasten the day of Christ's coming by obedient pioneering. He asked, "If we do that for every tribe, when will we get through? When are we going to reach the more than two thousand who do not have any Scripture in their language? We must pioneer."

Esther countered with how deeply she felt about the Piro's need for a training school, to which Townsend answered, "Esther, we must stick to pioneering. Let's pray that God will raise up someone else to assume this responsibility." How different the world picture might be today if more Christians had worked as wisely as Cameron Townsend.

Think of that future day when loud voices in heaven will say,

The kingdom of the world has become the kingdom of our Lord and of His Christ and He will be King forever (Rev. 11:15).

Think how long Christ has waited for us to finish our God-given task. Consider the millions who die with no knowledge of Him. As Jesus said, *"My food is to do what He wants who sent Me... and to finish His work"* (Jn. 4:34). Each believer should agree? "My aim is to help finish God's work."

You may remember Giuseppe Caribaldi, the military hero who fought to forge Italy into a single kingdom. His life was a series of ups and downs in several countries. During his final struggle to unite Italy, Garibaldi met one night in Rome with his volunteer "red shirts." As he stood before his ragged men, Garibaldi spoke simply of their common cause. Then he said,

I am going out from Rome. I offer neither quarters nor provisions nor wages. I offer hunger, thirst, forced marches, battles and death. Let him who loves me not with his head only but with his heart, follow me.

As one man, his men stepped forward.

Christ says to us, *"I'm going out from this land of light. I offer neither quarters nor provisions nor wages. I offer hunger, thirst, forced marches, battles and death. Let him who loves me not with his head only but with his heart, follow me."*

Will you step forward to follow Him? Be resolute in your commitment to help complete God's plan. His kingdom will come. Those who obey now will know fullness of joy in that hour. To work for Christ's coming kingdom is wise.

You would believe in

pioneer missions

if your family were a part of

an unevangelized people group.

As the Bible says:

"How beautiful is the coming

of those who bring good news."

-Rom. 10:15

Chapter Ten

Focus On The Finish

Brother Andrew, known to many as "God's Smuggler," relayed the following incident that happened to him when he spoke at a university in Alberta,

I opened the floor for questions and immediately two young men came from the back of the hall to the two microphones up front. Both were bearded fellows, dressed in a way that marked them as radicals.

They alternated in attacking Christians as racists and imperialists while praising Maoism and Marxism. Andrew finally cut them off and invited other students to speak or ask questions. But not one among the hundreds of Christian students responded, They were scared! The two radicals started again and seemingly couldn't be stopped.

Then, just when the situation seemed hopeless, two students, one black and one white, got up and walked to the microphones. The black student spoke first. "I am from Nigeria and I would like to take this opportunity to thank the Christians who came to Africa to tell us about Jesus Christ. If they had not come, I would not be at this university. I would still be a savage and a heathen. I would be lost forever, and I am so grateful that missionaries came to turn us away from this godless revolution."

The radical beside him looked silently down at his feet. Immediately the white student began to speak: He was a refu-

gee from Eastern Europe. "Because of the unbearable pressure from Communists, I was forced to flee my country. I am now free in this Christian country to do all the things I could not do in the land of my birth."

It was perfect. He went on to tell of communism and its repression of people. He ended by saying, "I am glad I am in a free society where everyone can speak, including the Marxist, because in my Marxist homeland anyone who spoke out against it was shot."

When he finished the crowd broke into applause and the radical students, without a word, almost ran out of the auditorium. Two Marxists intimidated four hundred Christians... because of the weakness of Christians, the silent majority.... This incident refutes the idea that communism is the church's number one enemy. There is a much bigger enemy than that: apathy. That is the greatest enemy. The battle can only be won by those who are willing to fight!

Christians Must Complete the Task

With two words, *"Follow Me,"* Christ summed up the Christian life. Significantly, he emphasized action. He did not say, "Think like I do," or "Have the right creed," or "Meditate daily." Those things are important, but they are not the crucial issue. To follow Christ means doing!

He gave us work to do in which He leads the way. He said:

If you serve Me, follow Me; and where I am, there My servant will be. If you serve Me, the Father will honor you (Jn. 12:26).

Ask yourself, "What better ambition could I have than to do my part in achieving Christ's objective?" Let that question float near the surface of your thinking. God's Son has made plain that:

The Christian should do something daily to help reach redemption's objective. Christ has ordered us to tell the good news of God's kingdom to everyone everywhere, then *"the end will come"* (Mt. 24:14). We must press toward the goal He has placed as our priority.

In Charles Dickens' famous story, "A Christmas Carol," one of the ghosts says to Scrooge, *"Mankind should be our business, Ebenezer; but we seldom attend to it."* God's plan targets all humanity. The Church must expand beyond its present boundaries. A church must be started in every people group. As soon as a people group has its church, the focus should shift to a group still unreached. People whose need is most pressing must always be priority one.

God's Gift is Incomparable

To offer eternal life to those *"dead in trespasses and sins"* is supremely important. Christ came to earth to *"save"* lost people (Lk. 19:10). Paul wrote of the grace of God that brings salvation (Tit. 2:11). All else is subordinate to eternal well-being.

General William Booth, founder of the Salvation Army, was a giant for God. He was far ahead of his generation in social planning. But William Booth was not satisfied to target purely physical needs. He summed up his convictions in these words:

Take a man out of the slums, heal his body, give him decent clothes, provide him a home in the country, then let him die and go to hell - really, it is not worthwhile.

The Gift Meets the Need of All

Salvation must be seen as primary. The angel said before Christ's birth,

You will call Him Jesus because He will save His people from their sins (Matt. 1:21).

Jesus declared, If anyone isn't born from above, he can't see God's Kingdom (Jn. 3:3).

That is the way home. Man's one hope of permanent well-being hinges on his relation to Jesus Christ. The Apostle Peter says,

No one else can save us, because in all the world there is only one name given us by which we must be saved (Acts 4:12).

The "good" can be the enemy of the "best" as we see in the many activities of churches. Lost people's deepest need is to be saved. That is not negotiable. To point people to Christ for salvation should be the priority of every church. Human destiny is an issue of life or death. Unreached peoples face being lost for eternity unless we give them the gospel. Words adapted from Leonard Ravenhill put it this way:

Could a mariner sit idle

If he heard the drowning cry?

Could a doctor sit in comfort

and just let his patients die?

Could a fireman sit idle,

let men burn and give no hand?

Can you sit at ease in Zion

with unreached peoples damned?

The Gift Must Be Offered to All

As Paul made it the purpose and passion of his life to give the gospel to those who knew nothing of Christ, so too must we. Paul believed the presence or absence of God's good news meant life or death. His words to the church elders as he was leaving Ephesus breathe commitment. Paul said,

I don't count my life worth anything. I just want to finish running my race and doing the work the Lord Jesus entrusted to me, declaring the good news of God's love (Acts 20:24).

Without salvation nothing has meaning.

Turn to Me to be saved, all you most distant parts of the world, because I am God and there is no other (Isa. 45:22).

This Old Testament statement agrees precisely with New Testament truth. Jesus said He came into the world to seek and to save that which was lost. He pointed out humanity's sole hope when He said, *"No one comes to the Father except by Me"* (Jn. 14:6).

Years ago, a picture was painted for the Royal Signal Corps of the British Army. It showed the lifeless body of one of their unarmed men in no man's land. A communication line had been cut by enemy shell fire and he had been sent to repair it.

Now stiff in death, his hands were holding the broken ends of the cable together. But the current was going through and communication had been restored. Under the picture was one word, "Contact." Sin cut the contact between unreachad people groups and God. Workers are needed to reestablish that communication. The life of every Christian who aids that effort could be summed up by the word, "Contact."

To Reach The Unreached Is Our Goal

At the dawn of our age of grace, Jesus prophesied,

This good news of the Kingdom must be preached all over the world so that all nations hear the truth. and then the end will come (Mt. 24:.14).

In order to fulfill that amazing prophecy, pioneering must be our major effort. William Borden of Yale died in Egypt on his way to the Orient as an ambassador for Christ. Borden said, *"If you see ten men trying to lift a log, nine of them on the light end and one on the heavy end, where will you step in to help?"* Common sense pleads for neglected peoples. Only pioneering expands God's kingdom.

Dr. Charles H. Kraft points out that though for generations we have looked to the Bible for our message, we have seldom looked to the Bible for our method. He states, "I have become convinced that the inspiration of the Bible extends both to message and to method." Why should a church not take Paul's missionary method as its model?

Pioneering Targets the Goal

A study of Romans 15:20-21 can help a church make a wise mid-course correction in order to redefine its target. The Apostle Paul says, *"Yea, so have I strived to preach the gospel not where Christ was named."* Paul's consistent method was to pioneer in new areas. The thought of *"strived,"* is accurately communicated by the word "ambition." Williams translates it, *"It has ever been my ambition..."* Vine's Expository Dictionary gives as synonyms: *"labor, endeavor, make it my aim."* God's revealed aim is to offer salvation to all our race. That became the focus of Paul's life. He built on that bedrock. It was his central thrust. To the Corinthians he declared, *"We'll tell the good news in the countries beyond you"* (II Cor. 10:16).

Supreme emphasis on pioneer evangelism is God's purpose for His people in this age of grace. God's method insures progress. Continuous growth will occur as we imitate Paul's plan. So long as our focus is to *"tell the good news only where Christ's name is not known,"* Christianity will expand.

The importance of applying this policy can hardly be exaggerated. Where churches are in decline, this focus will turn them around. It is the secret of success; the thrust we dare not dissipate. The only way God's kingdom can expand is by reaching and releasing Satan's captives.

Pioneer church planting accelerates that process. Pioneering means progress in world evangelism's final phase. It is right to concentrate our evangelical effort there.

Past Efforts Aimed at the Goal

Christianity's expansion is history's greatest success story. How does the world task stand today, almost nineteen hundred years downstream from the giving of the Great Commission?

Third world countries now sustain 18,000 cross cultural witnesses, a third as many as the United States and Canada support. When a government census in Japan asked, "Who is the greatest religious leader in history?" over seventy-five per cent of the respondents named Jesus Christ.

Korea has the largest church in the world and is perhaps the strongest Christian community in Asia. A third of lower level government officials say they are Christians. The proportion of Christians in the army and in upper echelons of government is even higher, almost fifty percent. Christians in Africa are increasing faster than the non-Christian population. In another decade the majority of Africa's population south of the Sahara may be Christian.

A trickle of Christians from the Western world has produced over 200 million Christians in non-western lands. Barrett's Encyclopedia lists over one hundred million in various Christian groups in Soviet Russia. Latin American evangelicals, a tiny group of 40,000 at the turn of the century, has, in the last two decades, become the world's fastest growing church now over 40 million strong. There were 2 million Christians in China when the Communists took over in 1949. Today believers there number at least 50 million.

Thus, Christianity has proved its power to flourish in almost any soil. In countless places it has taken root and grown spectacularly. Nevertheless, the world task is not done. It is too soon to quit.

Personal Issues Impact the Goal

In thousands of people groups Christianity has not yet been planted. Because each must have a church, you would be wise to shape your lifestyle to help finish the task. Is your way of life different because you believe that for people to know Christ is an issue of life or death? Would a Sunday visitor in your church note a wartime lifestyle? Why the strange barrier between what we believe and the way we live?

Even with our children grown, my wife and I find it hard to keep lifestyle consistent with our convictions. Four years ago, burglars looted our home. That influenced our decision to sell it and rent an apartment. It was a good move. Life is more simple. We can concentrate on concerns more meaningful than managing a house and yard.

What about wise use of money? Remember Jesus' exhortation,

With the money that's often used in wrong ways, win friends for yourselves so that when it's gone you'll be welcomed into the everlasting homes (Lk. 16:9).

Support of pioneer church planting should win us friends for eternity. Some Christians choose to have older cars. They can be well-maintained and still permit great savings in investment and insurance. Collision coverage can be avoided since even in the rare case of a car being "totalled," the replacement cost would not be prohibitive. By such lifestyle decisions thousands of dollars can be saved across the years to invest in world evangelization.

Should Christians leave a large estate? Jesus' command is to "...store up for your selves treasures in heaven..." (Mt. 6:20). Why not invest your assets in the world's highest priority task? My wife and I hope to die poor. As a policy we have sought at Christmas to give our children a cash gift instead of a future inheritance. They are grateful and support our aim to have the bulk of our assets go to pioneer outreach for Christ. This way they may also be less eager for us to die! Our hope is that we will neither leave excess money at our death nor be a financial burden to our children in our last years.

Whatever you decide about these and similar matters, make God's world plan the touchstone of all you do. As surely as God lives, His plan is for His people to finish world evangelization.

Pace Setters Go For the Goal

The affirmation produced by young people at the Edinborough World Evangelization Conference in 1980 says it well:

By the grace of God and for His glory, I commit my entire life to obeying His commission of Matthew 28:18-20, wherever, and however He leads me, giving priority to the peoples currently beyond reach of the gospel (Rom. 15:20-21). I will also endeavor to impart this vision to others.

Will you live by those guidelines? To do so is apt to bring you into contact with workers for Christ who will inspire you. It is a privilege to stand behind the pace-setters.

A letter came not long ago from a friend working in a difficult people group. He says, *"Several days ago I was very nearly killed by a mob of enraged Bengali villagers who mistook me for a robber."* He was alone at night on a very bumpy dirt road waiting for a man who had gone on a brief errand. Suddenly he was aware of shouts and screams coming from a village close by. He tried to drive away but someone saw the van and screamed, *"There go the robbers!"* Just then his progress was blocked by an ox cart. In moments he was surrounded by dozens of screaming Bengalis. The windshield was smashed; he was dragged from the car as the chant was raised, *"Kill him! Kill him! Kill him!"* He was slammed to his knees and beaten. One man plunged a spear into his arm. Soon his glasses, watch and car keys were gone. The man he was waiting for got some unarmed constables. As they ran up he was struck on his left eye. With great effort, he was rescued and released from the mob.

My friend added that for some time he had felt his love for the Lord had been growing cold and he had been praying for its renewal. After his beating as he went to get medical aid, he began to weep. He said:

I could see Jesus on the road to the cross. I could see Him being beaten, spat upon, struck and hated. For the first time in my life I think I could really feel just what He had suffered to save me from my sins. And no one came to His rescue.

Apathy Guards the Goal

God does sustain those who have counted the cost to serve Him in far places. Are their efforts vain? Indeed not. Small groups of Bengali believers have come into being. The gospel is changing lives. God's Word gives fruit. Believers will emerge from *"every kindred and tongue and people and nation."*

Let each ask, "What price am I paying to finish our God-given task?" Perhaps you agree God intends each church to focus on unreached peoples. You believe that to extend God's kingdom is the main thing. What then? Will you get involved? Change your giving? Redirect your influence? Consider going? In God's plan it is essential that His people completely evangelize the world.

It is easier to serve God without a vision,

easier to work for God without a call,

because then you are not bothered
by what God requires;

common sense is your guide,
veneered over with Christian sentiment.

But if once you receive a commission
from Jesus Christ,

the memory of

<u>what God wants</u>

will always come like a goad;

and you will no longer be able
to work for Him

on the common sense basis.

-Oswald Chambers

Chapter Eleven

Godlike Giving

Selfishness can be deadly. One day, toward the close of World War II in a fashionable western home, the phone rang. The woman who answered heard the words, "Hi, Mom, I'm coming home." It was her sailor son just back from active duty. He was calling from San Diego. The mother was wild with joy. Her son was alive. He went on, I'm bringing a buddy with me. He got hurt pretty bad. Only has one eye, one arm and one leg. He has no home and I'd sure like him to live with us."

The mother said, "Sure, son, he can stay with us for awhile."

"Mom, you don't understand. I want him to live with us always."

Said the mother, "Well, OK, we'll try it for a year."

"But, Mom, I want him to be with us always. He's in bad shape, one eye, one arm, one leg."

The mother got impatient. "Son, you're too emotional about this. You've been in a war. The boy will be a drag on us."

The phone clicked, and went dead. The next day the parents received a telegram from the Navy. Their son had leaped to his death from the twelfth floor of a San Diego hotel. In a few days the body was shipped home. When the casket was opened the parents stared at their son's body. He had one eye, one arm and one leg. With crushing pain came understanding. Fearing rejection, their son had phoned seeking acceptance. His mother's unwillingness to show love and bear a burden had snapped his fragile will to live.

Selfishness is not simply unattractive. It is deadly. And it affects a Christian's attitude toward giving. For that reason this chapter might be the most important in this book.

To the degree a believer must be pressured to support God's work, his motives are wrong. He fails to understand why God wants him to give.

My thoughts are not your thoughts, and your ways are not My ways, says the Lord (Is. 55:8).

Therefore, we need to know why the believer should be a glad and radical giver. These truths may revolutionize one's stewardship practices. Surprisingly, the Bible affirms you should:

Live In Order To Give

On the face of it that statement seems to need qualifying. Surely everybody can't give. We argue that some don't have enough to give anything. Also it should be clear that the more you give the less you have, and obviously that would be bad, or so we reason. But, no, the Bible affirms the opposite. It declares the more you give the more you gain. As an old epitaph put it:

Give and you will gain, keep and you will lose is a law of the universe. Thus, the Bible urges and encourages radical giving.

God Seeks Radical Givers

The Bible does not present a "common sense" approach to giving. To share moderately while being careful to "watch out for number one" does not reflect the Bible's teaching on this important subject. Extreme giving is recommended in God's Word and unexpected results are promised. By precept, starting in the Old Testament, God tells us what to do and the results that will follow. Wise King Solomon declares, for example:

Be generous to others and you'll grow prosperous; refresh others and you'll be refreshed (Pr.11:25).

Jesus' teaching on giving is radical, as when He says,

Give, and it will be given you. A good measure, pressed together, shaken down, and running over will be put into your lap. You see the measure you use will be used for you (Lk. 6:38).

The Apostle Paul declares,

We should help the weak and remember what the Lord Jesus said: "We are more blessed when we give than when we receive" (Acts 20:35).

To this exhortation urging extreme giving, Paul adds,

Remember this: If you sow little, you won't get much grain. But if you sow generously, you will get much grain (II Cor. 9:6).

So the Bible teaches that by giving one will become richer. By giving we will receive.

Giving to Needs Falls Short

At this point we must ask ourselves why we give to the Church. Do we think we are meeting God's needs? If we think so we are wrong. Many Christians are moved to contribute because they believe that God or His work have needs they can supply. That may be our thought, but it is not God's. Theologians remind us that if God lacks anything then He is not God. Hear Him say:

Listen, My people, ...I do not criticize you for your sacrifices, for regularly bringing Me your burnt offerings. But I need not take a bull from your homes or a he-goat from your folds, since all the animals in the forest are mine and the cattle on the hills by the thousand... If I were hungry I need not tell you because the world is Mine and everything in it (Ps. 50:7-12).

God lacks nothing nor does He want us to give because we think He seeks such help. The Apostle Paul confirms that:

[God] isn't served by human hands as if He needed anything. He Himself gives everyone life and breath and everything (Acts 17:25).

Yet Jesus Christ spoke often of giving and always as though it were enormously important. He patiently sought to impart to His followers God's perspective. In broad terms, it may be summarized as follows:

As living to give blesses, so living to get curses.

Giving and Getting Involve Divine Laws

These laws operate negatively and positively. The Bible warns,

Don't make a mistake; you can't fool God. Whatever you sow, you'll reap. If you sow to please your own flesh, you will from your flesh reap destruction (Gal.6:7-8).

When men and women reject God's Spirit in order to sow evil they reap a harvest of destruction. King Adoni-bezek fought a losing battle against Israel, then fled. They pursued and caught him, then cut off his thumbs and his big toes. Adoni-bezek said,

Seventy kings with their thumbs and big toes cut off used to pick up food under my table. As I did, so God paid me back (Judg. 1:7).

Gehazi, servant of Elisha, was another man who chose to get instead of to give. By deceit he got merchandise and a quantity of silver. But Elisha unmasked Gehazi's falseness with the words:

Is this a time to take money and to take clothes, olive orchards and vineyards, sheep, cattle, servants, and maids? And so Naaman's leprosy will cling to you and your descendants forever. When he left him, he was leprous, as white as snow (2 Kgs. 5:26-27).

Ananias in the early church was even more sternly judged. He wanted to get, while posing as a giver. But he was confronted with his wickedness by the Apostle Peter who asked,

"How could you think of doing such a thing? You didn't lie to men but to God!" When Ananias heard him say this, he fell down and died (Acts 5:5-6).

Selfishness is not simply unattractive, it, is a deadly enemy. See it for what it is.

Give so God's Law Will Bless You

The positive side of God's law operates with equal certainty.

Whatever you sow, you'll reap ... If you sow to please the Spirit, you will from the Spirit reap everlasting life (Gal. 6:7-8).

Wise people set aside what they want in order to do what God wants. His infinite riches are ours to enjoy when we yield our puny selves and possessions to Him. Take the case of Abraham. God blessed him greatly, saying, *"...in you all the people in the world will be blessed" (Gen.12:3).* What mind-boggling words! God promised worldwide salvation through Abraham. *"In your Descendant all the people on earth will be blessed"* (Gen. 22:18).

Notice carefully the Holy Spirit's New Testament commentary on those texts. The Apostle Paul wrote,

The Bible foresaw that God would make the nations righteous by faith, and long ago He told Abraham the good news: "Through you all nations will be blessed" (Gal. 3:8).

Yes, God blessed Abraham tremendously, but also asked him for his best. As the Bible says, *"God tested Abraham."*

Abraham had waited long for the son God had promised him. His faith had been stretched again and again. But at last Isaac was born and in time became a strapping young man. Through Isaac all God's promises to Abraham were to be fulfilled. Then the blow fell. God told Abraham to take Isaac to the country of Moriah and sacrifice him there as a burnt offering. Abraham obeyed; the two went together to the place of sacrifice. Abraham built an altar, arranged the wood, bound Isaac and laid him on the wood. Finally, we see the father standing, knife in raised fist, ready to plunge it into the heart of his son. At that moment a voice from heaven calls him,

Don't lay your hands on the boy... Now I know you fear God: You didn't refuse to give Me your only son (Gen. 22:12).

Because Abraham was willing to give all to God, he got all God had for him. Whether or not to take God's way is our choice. God wants us to live to give.

Give Because You Are God's Child

We should give because we are God's children and have His nature. This is the most valid reason for us to be radically generous givers. Such giving satisfies His expectation of us as His children.

In Genesis we hear Him say:

Let us make man in Our image, like Ourselves, that they might rule over the fish in the sea, the birds in the air, and the cattle, over all the earth and everything that moves on the earth (Gen. 1:26).

God deeply desires to have His children resemble Him. The Apostle Paul writes,

You are all God's children by believing in Christ Jesus, because all of you who were baptized into Christ have put on Christ (Gal. 3:26).

God wants His children to think as Christ Jesus thought:

Although He was God, He decided not to take advantage of His being equal with God as though it were stolen goods, but He emptied Himself, made Himself a slave, became like other human beings, and was seen to have the ways of a man. He became obedient and humbled Himself till He died, yes, died on a cross (Phil. 2:6-8).

Give With the Future in View

God wants us rich forever. Most "getting " is short-term. Thus, Paul warns us against attachment to things that are temporary, saying,

We don't look at the things that are seen but at the things that are not seen. What we see lasts only a while, but what we don't see lasts forever (II Cor. 4:18)

Again the scriptures record,

So don't feel proud of men. You see, everything is yours, Paul, Apollos, Peter; the world, life or death, present or future things, everything is yours, but you belong to Christ, and Christ to God (I Cor. 3:21-23).

Riches acquired by getting are short-lived. They cannot last. My friends Greg and Sally Livingstone were in the home of a wealthy woman. The mansion was filled with beautiful antique furniture. Greg and Sally "oohed and aahed" with appreciation. The owner of the priceless antiques shrugged and said, "It's just furniture, honey." Later that day Greg and his wife learned the woman had terminal cancer and knew she would soon die. They thought of her words, "It's just furniture, honey." Said Greg, "Those words are one of the greatest sermons I ever heard."

Aren't you glad God wants to give us things we will enjoy forever? *"Incorruptible," "undefiled,"* and "unfading" are words that Peter uses to describe them (1 Pet. 1:4 KJV).

How sad that more people do not adopt God's perspective given us in His Word. A Los Angeles Times news item last year reported: "Stuart Kelly died of cancer Sunday night, six months and fifteen days after he had won $14,000,000." The article went on to tell that the fifty-seven year old truck driver had only possessed the then record lottery jackpot a short time when he learned he had cancer. He died six months later. Fourteen million dollars, to that time the largest lottery prize in North American history, meant little in the face of death. There was no way Kelly could take it with him.

We must turn from the siren lure of "getting" in order to practice radical giving. The Bible suggests that giving with a spirit of joy is evidence of a relationship with God. As the Apostle John teaches, "We *love because He first loved us*" *(1 Jn. 4:19). So too, "We give because He first gave to us."*

God Models the Giving He Asks

The best known verse in the Bible pictures it:

God so loved the world that He gave His only-begotten Son so that whoever believes in Him might not perish but have everlasting life (Jn. 3:16)

God's love is a great mystery. We talk of it without understanding. We are like little children on the floor around a
newspaper reading the figures of our United States national
debt. The children can spell out the words and read the numbers but with no idea of their meaning. So it is with our at-
tempts to fathom the mystery of God's love for us. That un-
quenchable yearning to redeem lost humanity may be the
reason God's name is love. The Bible declares,

*He saved us and called us to be holy, not because we did
anything, but because He planned a gift of His grace and
gave it to us in Christ Jesus before the world began (II Tim.
1:9). Appointed before the world was made, He was revealed
in the last period of time to help you (I Peter 1:20). The
Lamb... was sacrificed before history began (Rev. 13:8).*

God's love for our race is from eternity and to eternity.

God gave Himself for us in Christ

Paul puts it so well, saying,

*In Christ, God was getting rid of the enmity between Him-
self and the people of the world by not counting their sins
against them, and He has put into our hands the message
how God and men are made friends again (II Cor.5:19).*

Some say they don't understand that. But it's not hard.
Suppose you are a parent whose child is being operated on.
You see your child passing under the influence of the anesthetic as the operation is about to begin. The child is moving
out of his fear and suffering, but you are moving into yours!
And the surgeon's knife goes deeper into you than into your
child's flesh.

And when he comes out from under the anesthetic and the
pain begins to write itself on his face: Oh, my friend, how it

writes itself on your own heart. And you feel far more the pain than if it were in your own body. Yes, our heavenly Father *"...didn't spare His own Son, but gave Him up for all of us"* (Rom. 8:32).

My wife and I will never forget a painful experience we suffered while living in Argentina One of our sons, Peter, four years old, was stricken with measles. His abdomen grew hard, as though his lower body were paralyzed. We got the best specialist available. He called in others. The result was a four hour exploratory operation.

At last the doctor came out of the operating theater. The specialist told us "I'm sorry. There's nothing we can do. The fluids in your son's body have auto-digested the pancreas. He can't live without a pancreas.

I said, "Doctor, how long can he last?"

"Perhaps forty-eight hours," he said. Agonizingly, I endured those seemingly endless hours. Peter's pain somehow became a part of me, merging with my utter anguish. At last the ordeal was over. And Peter was still alive. Our son's life was miraculously spared. That experience convinced me, however, that to identify fully with another's pain is possible.

In Christ, God was getting rid of the enmity between Himself and the people of the world. In the agony of Calvary's cross, God gave Himself.

Christ Gave Himself for Us

We know also that Christ gave Himself voluntarily. As He approached the cross He dismissed the idea that He was a victim He said,

The Father loves Me because I give My life in order to take it back again. Nobody takes it from Me No, of My own free will I am giving it. I have the power to give it, and I have the power to take it back again (Jn,10:17-18).

The apostle Paul put it in a different way when he said,

You know the grace of our Lord Jesus Christ. He was rich, but became poor for you to make you rich by His poverty (II Cor. 8:9).

We think it amazing when a person gives his life for a friend. As Christ said, "No one has greater love than he who gives his life for his friends" (Jn.15:13). God's Son laid down His life for His enemies, for those who hated Him and spit upon Him. No wonder Paul wrote,

But God shows how he loves us by this, that while we were still sinners Christ died for us (Rom.5:8).

God Encourages Radical Giving

As we give, our ability to appropriate Christ increases. John says,

This is how we learned what love is: He gave His life for us. We too should give our lives for our fellow Christians (I Jn. 3:16).

Paul speaks to this intimate experience in the words, "...for me to live is Christ and to die is gain" (Phil, 1:21). And again,

I don't live any more, but Christ lives in me. The life I now live in my body I live by believing in the Son of God who loved me and gave Himself for me (Gal. 2:20).

To understand what John and Paul meant by the words just quoted helps to unlock the meaning of Jesus' statement, *"It is more blessed to give than to receive"* (Acts 20:35 KJV). What the Apostle Paul was saying also becomes evident,

If you sow little, you won't get much grain. But if. you sow generously, you will get much grain. Everyone should do what he has made up his mind to do, not with regret or being forced, because God loves anyone who gives gladly (II Cor. 9:6-7)

I heard Stanford Kelly tell an incident from Haiti where he lived for years. Bear in mind that Haiti is one of the poorest countries in the world.

The church was having a Thanksgiving festival and each Christian was invited to bring a love offering. One envelope from a Haitian man named Edmund held $13 cash. That amount was three months' income for a working man there. Kelly was as surprised as those counting a Sunday offering in the United States might be to get a $6,000 cash gift. He looked around for Edmund, but couldn't see him.

Later Kelly met him in the village and questioned him. He pressed him for an explanation and found that Edmund had sold his horse in order to give the $13 gift to God. But why hadn't he come to the festival? He hesitated and didn't want to answer.

Finally Edmund said, "I had no shirt to wear."

Here was a man who loved Christ. Though he had no shirt and thus felt unable to join the other Christians at the church, he gave three months' wages in a single gift.

Edmund understood God's heart. He was obeying Christ's word,

Store up for yourselves treasures in heaven, where no moth or rust destroys and no thieves break in and steal (Mt. 6:20).

Kelly went on to explain how he had told this incident in different American churches. After one meeting a richly dressed woman came to him, drew three dollars from her purse, and asked him to use the money to buy Edmund a shirt. Kelly was disappointed.

He looked the woman squarely in the eye and said, "I didn't tell you what Edmund did to get you to give three dollars to buy him a shirt. I did it to encourage you to do something for God that would mean as much to you as Edmund's gift meant to him."

Edmund understood the reason for giving; the woman did not.

Because God is the great Giver and you are His child, He profoundly longs for you to live in order to give. His love saturates His will for your well-being. Choose the extreme giving He models as the central thrust of your life.

The more you give,

the more you will please God

and the more you will have forever.

Christ's Great Commission
offers but two options:

obedience
and endless blessing,
or disobedience
and endless sorrow.

"Let me assure you, " Jesus said,
"everyone who gave up his home,
brothers or sisters, mother, father,
or children, or fields for me
and for the good news,
will certainly get a hundred times
as much here in this life:
houses, brothers and sisters,
mothers and children and fields,
with persecutions,
and in the coming world
everlasting life.
But many who are first
will be last,
and the last
first."

- Mk. 10:29-31

Chapter Twelve

Success By Grace

Playing tennis with an insurance executive one day, I invited him to visit Pakistan with me.

"When are you going?" he asked.

"In two months."

Things worked out for him and we spent three weeks together in that fascinating land. He said later the trip transformed his life. Evidence of the gospel's life-changing power almost overwhelmed him. The commitment of believers who were reaching out to others with the love of Christ affected him beyond words. He said simply, "On the long flight from Karachi back to London, I was so moved I had to keep wiping away the tears. It was embarrassing, yet I couldn't help myself."

You, too, can experience more of that kind of reality. I encourage you to go for true success – by God's grace. As you read this last chapter, you may be asking, "What now?" Perhaps you are convinced already that God's command to *"Go"* means you. But how to obey? How to please God? What to do?

Here is a simple self-test that will help you go forward :

Do what will give you joy on the judgment day. Do now what at the last hour you will wish you had done. The Apostle Paul declares, *"...each of us will have to give an account of himself to God"* (Rom. 14:12). More explicitly he says that each will *"...receive according to what he has done ..."* (II Cor. 5:10). God requires you to respond, to be a *"doer."*

A student at the New York Institute of Advertising was explaining why he had chosen the advertising field;

He said, "I have dreams of making a million dollars in advertising just like my father."

The teacher asked, "When did your father make a million dollars in advertising?"

"Oh, he didn't," said the student, "but he had dreams too." Dreaming is one thing, doing is another. Mark the difference as you hunger to improve.

One of these days, should my Lord not come first, I'll die. That will mean I am with Jesus Christ. *"To be absent from the body"* is to be *"present with the Lord"* (II Cor. 5:8 KJV). Should you hear that news, I hope you will say, "Norm's gratitude to God for His grace made him work to do what God wanted done."

Near the end of Jesus' teaching time He said to His disciples, "If you know this, you're happy if you DO it" (Jn. 13:17). Jesus repeatedly emphasized doing. The Apostle James added,

Always do what the Word says; don't merely listen to it and so deceive yourselves (Jas. 1:22).

Settle the fact in your heart that you must...

Obey to Succeed

Note the author of Hebrews' strong words:

Although Jesus is the Son, He found out from what He suffered what it means to obey. And when He was finished

He became One who gives everlasting salvation to all who obey Him (Heb. 5:8-9).

The same author affirmed, *"You can't please God without faith"* (Heb. 11:6). Faith always produces faith-works. *"Faith without works is dead"* (Jas.2:26). Only that trust which causes action pleases God. True faith will make you a doer for God.

Even the non-Christian world is impressed when saying what one believes is balanced by doing. Julius Caesar was not only a great soldier and statesman but a great speaker. Once after he spoke in the Roman Forum, Cicero, one of the greatest orators of ancient times, said, "He speaks as well as any professional orator who does nothing but make speeches. And look what he does besides!"

What the Christian must do to succeed is evident in Paul's praise of the churches of Macedonia for what they did. He tells of their *"overflowing joy and generosity"* even *"while they were severely tested by trouble"* and in *"deep poverty."* Then Paul adds that they had *"given all they could, yes, more than they could give."* He aptly summarizes,

They did more than we expected: they gave themselves to the Lord first and then to us, doing just what God wanted (II Cor 8:5).

Those Christians committed themselves to Christ and to His world evangelization priority by linking up with Paul's evangelistic church planting team. You can imitate them today as you:

Yield to God to Succeed

"They gave themselves to the Lord first." Surrender to Christ is key to all the riches God has for you. His loving

invitation covers all that any troubled heart could desire. Notice carefully how complete His promise is. He pleads:

Come to Me, all you who are working hard and carrying a heavy load, and I will give you rest. Take My yoke on you, and learn from Me. I am gentle and humble minded, then you will find your rest. My yoke is easy and My load is light (Mt. 11:28-30).

To know the depth of one's need and to discover that Christ is the answer is the start of success.

Your first need is to yield yourself wholly to Christ. Think of it this way, "World evangelization is me." Count on God; do what you can. Remember Isaiah the prophet's experience. He seems to have been tuned-in to God, listening. At any rate he overheard a conversation among the members of the Godhead. He writes,

I heard the Lord ask, "Whom should I send and who will go for us" Then I said, "Here am I. Send me" (Isa. 6:8).

Put yourself unreservedly in God's hands. As Paul says,

Don't let sin keep on using your body as a tool for doing wrong. But as people who have come back from the dead and live, give yourselves to God, and let God use your body as a tool for doing what is right (Rom.6:13).

Commitment Means Change

It will cause changes in what you do. Growth comes as you bring Christ into your daily life. His command is simply, *"Follow Me."* Focus and re-focus on Christ. As David put it,

I always keep the Lord before me. With Him at my right hand, I can't fail (Ps. 16:8).

Put yourself under the authority of the Bible. Start each day in God's Word, asking Him to apply its truth to your life.

Is it too much to read daily three and a half pages in the Old Testament and one page in the New Testament? With most Bibles that amount each day will take you through it all in a year. If you are really hungry for God's Word, double the recipe and read seven Old Testament pages and two New Testament pages daily. Your life will improve as the Bible goes through you and you through it twice a year. Read the Bible avidly. Why? You need its power working in you to change you. You must have it! D.L. Moody once said, "I never saw a useful Christian who was not a student of the Bible."

To develop self-discipline is a challenge. Avoid the television habit with its power to force you into the world's mold. How appropriate are the Psalmist's words,

Turn my eyes away from watching worthless things. By Your power give me a new life (Ps. 119:37).

Read good books. Get into the lives of men and women who have lived for world evangelization.

Seek opportunities in your church to strengthen its outreach to the world. Should you not find support for pioneer evangelism in its program, seek those who will help you launch something. Your effort will please God. Obey Him, for His grace guarantees your success.

You may say, "How will I know what to do?" When Mr. J. L. Kraft, the cheese manufacturer, was asked the reason for his success, he said, "The ability to make up my mind." He explained,

When I have a decision to make, first I pray hard. Then I think hard, and when time is about up and I must have the answer, I say, "Lord, now You show me the next thing to do." Then the first idea that comes into my mind after I have gone through that process is what I take to be the answer. I have been correct a large enough percentage of the time to per-suade me that this course is sound.

If the Bible is the basis for the hard thinking and praying Kraft practices, his method seems sound. Stay in God's Word, pray hard; think hard; then act.

Commitment Activates Grace

The test of this book is whether after reading it your ac-tual behavior becomes more pleasing to God. Keep counting on God's grace. Ask our Lord each morning to make you effective as His ambassador in the world task. You cannot succeed simply by self-effort. You will face opposition if you support pioneer work because it is the cutting edge of God's program. The devil will resist you, but God's work is worth your best effort.

Nathan Hale, Revolutionary War hero who died as a spy, said at the last, "My only regret is that I have but one life to give for my country." One life! Make yours count for Christ's "Priority One."

That is not to say you must simply grit your teeth and plow ahead. No matter how much self-discipline you have, it will fall short. Do your best, yes. But always picture yourself floating in an ocean of God's grace.

Commit your ways to the Lord, trust Him, and He will act [for you] (Ps. 37:5).

Wonderful is the grace of God!

The late Dr. A.J. Gordon, founder of Gordon College and gifted pastor, did not live to old age. As he faced death, he felt his work for God was of small value. In his final hours, he asked to be left alone for a time with his Lord. Those outside the closed door could hear his pleading prayer and the sobs that shook him as he was brought low in God's holy presence. Gordon did not fear death but felt that his life, which others regarded so highly, was of little worth in the sight of God. Dr. Gordon's experience is a reminder that God's pure, undeserved grace underlies all our faith-works. It is the bed-rock of all our hope.

Push God's Priority to Succeed

Paul writes, *"They gave themselves... to us, doing just what God wanted."* Participation with pioneers working beyond Christian boundaries still counts with God as it did in Paul's time. The Macedonian believers *"gave themselves"* to the church planting band led by the Apostle Paul. To do that with a similar team today is equally appropriate and pleasing to God.

Give What You Have

Give generously to that work. Faith's primary test always focuses on what you have. You must give account of your assets to God. Remember how He got Moses out of Egypt and into the desert. Finally, God got his attention and asked, *"What is that in your Hand?"* (Ex. 4:2). *"A rod,"* Moses answered. Then God showed him he could do wonderful things with what he had in his hand. Do you see? God asks an account of your possessions, the assets you have now.

It was like that with the widow of a prophet in Israel. She told Elisha her husband was dead and a creditor was about to take her two children as slaves.

"What should I do for you?" Elisha asked her. *"Tell me, what do you have in your house?"* *"Your maid has nothing in the house except a jar of olive oil,"* she answered (II Kgs 4:2).

With that olive oil Elisha solved her problems and gave her family a future with hope.

Jesus also taught His disciples that if they would trust Him with what they had, He would multiply it for the blessing of many.

A crowd once followed them into the desert. When evening came the disciples asked Jesus to send the people away to the villages to buy food. Jesus answered them,

"They don't need to go away. You give them something to eat." "All we have here is five loaves and two fish," they told Him. "Let Me have them," He said and He ordered the people to sit down on the grass. Then taking the five loaves and the two fish and looking up to heaven, He blessed them. Breaking the loaves He gave them to the disciples, and they gave them to the people (Mt. 14:16-20).

Give What You Earn

Note Jesus' words, *"Let Me have them."* What wisdom for us to imitate in managing our assets! Give Him what you have now.

One of the most commonly ignored commands of Jesus is this,

I tell you, with the money that's often used in wrong ways, win friends for yourselves so that when it's gone you'll be welcomed into the everlasting homes (Lk.16:9).

What was Jesus' highest use for money? To save people, to give them eternal life. How well do Christians support that work? In a study of church giving in the United States, John Holzmann states, "North American evangelicals are frontier mission minded at a rate of less than a nickel per $100." Money can send pioneer workers but only when given.

Are you aware that scores of new workers are ready to go right now but lack travel funds? The problem is shockingly huge. Many sending agencies must ask candidates to raise money for their passage and support overseas. It is hard, slow work because so many believers are only "token" givers. Is it fair to treat young workers thus as our response to their willingness to go to unreached peoples? Obedient giving would meet their need.

How different it is when Christians care. Eight families belonging to a mainline denomination in Indianapolis became interested in witness abroad. They found an overseas worker who needed a bicycle, and together they bought it for him. The next year they pooled funds to buy him a wristwatch. Then they visited a church with a vision for outreach abroad. Each family made a faith promise to give a certain amount each week. Five years later, those eight families were giving $25,000 annually for world evangelization. From a bicycle a year to $25,000 a year based on better motivation!

Give With Wisdom

Money given wisely is a key to expanding God's kingdom beyond present frontiers.

Don Rubesh, who died recently, helped spread the gospel by radio in India. Christians in the west gave largely to support daily gospel broadcasts to blanket an area where three hundred million Hindi-speaking people live. That work produced a huge harvest with many thousands being saved.

If no money had been given, no gospel would have been broadcast. If part had been given, a partial harvest would have resulted. If more had been given, can we doubt more would have been saved?

Give yourself to agencies whose focus is right. Seek agencies who send people to start churches in people groups who have none. Find organizations whose principal thrust is to extend Christ's kingdom beyond present boundaries. Coach (Bear) Bryant, sometimes called the "winningest coach in history," took football teams to twelve bowl games in thirteen years. Bryant gives this counsel:

Decide what you want to do, pick an endeavor. Then formulate a plan to reach the goal and tie yourself to persons who believe in that plan. Tie yourself to a leader, a self-starter, a person who says, "Let's go. "

And you have to learn to fight. I don't mean a fist fight. If you're forty years old, your house is burned down, the bank has turned down a loan and your wife has run off with a drunk, you'd better be ready to fight.

Helping a team bring a church into being in a land where God's good news is scarcely known will face you with a different kind of fight.

You're not fighting against flesh and blood but against the rulers, authorities, and lords of this dark world, against the evil spirits that are above (Eph.6:12).

But there is no better battle in which to fight.

Keep God's "Priority One" as your own. More current than tomorrow's news are Christ's words, *"Seek ye first the Kingdom of God"* (Mt. 6:33 KJV).

Give While You Live

Jim Elliot, martyred for Christ in Ecuador, said,

Live so that when you come to die you will have nothing to do but die.

God's rescue operation for a lost world is the best enterprise on earth. As God enlarges your vision of far fields you will appreciate how varied the needs are. My father was a businessman. When he was sixty, he visited French West Africa where the gospel was transforming thousands of lives. His heart was thrilled by the proof of God's power, but he was grieved over illnesses of workers caused by lack of dental care. Deeply burdened, my father studied dentistry and later returned to Africa with a dental clinic. He met the dental needs of over 700 Christian workers. Giving himself unsparingly to that work, he went twice to Africa then to Latin America and to the Orient to improve the health of God's workers. That effort filled the last fifteen years of his life. A few days before he died at age seventy-nine he said to me, "Norman, I'm not afraid to die. But I've so much wanted to live for there is so much to be done."

But to hasten the coming of God's kingdom does not always require going abroad. Far from it. Scores of organizations (like the one I work with) have places for many people. Far more could be done to extend God's kingdom if more people would volunteer.

Why not make a change? Why not use the rest of your life doing things you'll be glad for when you face eternity?

Most who read these words could be involved fully in work whose effects will last forever. The price? Willingness perhaps to live a simpler lifestyle. Middle-aged or retired Christians could provide solid help at the home base of a sending agency. A letter to me at the address at the close of this book will bring you information.

Give All

Today it is practical to visit distant places where pioneer work is being done. Others are extending God's kingdom and you can join forces with them.

I like Al Wheeler's story. He serves Christ in the jungles of Colombia. In his remote village mail is dropped periodically by parachute from a plane. One day, he got a letter from the University of California at Berkeley. The university wanted to publish a book of success stories of alumni. Since Al had a Ph.D. from there, they wanted his story.

Enclosed was the following survey:

1. "Do you own your own home?" Al looked at the two-room mud hut he was in and said, "Well, yes! I paid for this with a hundred dollars' worth of machetes and trinkets. Yes, I own my own home."

2. "Do you own a second home?" Al thought, "I sure do! Back at the jungle advance base station there is a one-room mud hut that we have things stored in. Yes, I have a second home."

3. "Do you own a boat?" He looked out through the open hole in the wall that served as a window. In the moonlight, he could see the dugout canoe he had bought from the Indians. He said, "Yes, I own my own boat."

4. "What is your salary'!" This was a multiple choice question with a salary beginning at $250,000 and going down from there. Al went down the choices but the last was still nowhere near as low as his income so he crossed it out and put down his small salary.

5. "Are you traveling abroad this year?" With furlough coming up he could write, "Yes, we are traveling abroad this year." With a chuckle he thought, "I can hardly wait till this letter gets back to the school's computer!"

Al's is not the typical success story, but his is the success that counts with God. And you can be part of the cause to which he is committed.

Jesus said of Mary, who poured the costly perfume on His head, *"She hath done what she could..."* (Mk.14:8 KJV). No one could want a better commendation from Jesus than that,

"He has done what he could"

"She has done what she could"

Remember, the proof of faith is faith-works. Move ahead doing things that will give you joy on the judgment day. And know that to the believer who obeys God, His grace guarantees success.

BEFORE YOU PUT THIS BOOK DOWN

Assuming you have stayed with me to this point, I can't quite let you go. Not yet

For you the most valuable pages in this book may be those just ahead. Why? Because they offer open doors you may walk through into a wider, more wonderful experience in Christ.

What follows is not an exhaustive catalogue of Christian agencies. Instead, I recommend these few organizations to you for special reasons. I hope you will contact one or more of them for the help I believe they can be to you.

Norm Lewis

FRONTIERS

I have worked with Frontiers since it was launched in 1982. We now have over 200 members. Ours is an innovative interdenominational faith mission agency, working closely with local churches established throughout the Muslim world. Frontiers' 20 year goal is 2,000 committed ambassadors for Christ planting churches among 200 Muslim people groups

Norm Lewis

"Frontiers is looking for people who are ready to 'go for it' We covet committed Christians who will keep on until mature believers abound throughout the Muslim world. The vast majority of peoples today who have NO church live under governments who will not issue missionary visas. But our Lord did not say, 'Make disciples of all nations if you can get a missionary visa.' He did say, 'I will build my church and the gates of Hell will not prevail against it' (Matt.16:18). We believe this is God's hour for the Muslim world. For the person unable to serve abroad, wonderful opportunities for service here in the U.S. are open. Contact us today."

Greg Livingstone, Founder-Director

P.O. Box 40159, 1610 Elizabeth St., Pasadena. CA 91104

(818) 798-0807

6240 London Road, Richmond, BC,V7E 3S4, Canada

P.O. Box 351,CH-9424 Rheineck. Switzerland

OPERATION MOBILIZATION

I admire Operation Mobilization for its effectiveness in harnessing the energies of multitudes of youth cross-culturally in world evangelization. Over the years, more than 90,000 young people have been impacted by God while with OM. Founded in 1957, the ministry has grown from a handful of students to approximately 2600 full time workers and an additional 4000+ short term volunteers annually from all over the world. OM focuses on the Muslim world, and urban areas and also has a fruitful literature ministry to port cities all over the world with their two ships, Doulos and Logos II. I would covet for every Christian a short term, cross-cultural, life changing experience with Operation Mobilization.

Norm Lewis

Your part in world mission

You may be asking where you, as a Christian, fit into God's plan for the salvation of the world. Here are a few ways you can be Involved now!

YOU CAN PRAY - Get informed about God's world. Ask for information about missionaries in areas of particular interest to you. Stand before God on behalf of your brothers and sisters on the mission field. Pray for more missionaries to be called and sent to reach the lost for Christ. Don't be surprised if God uses you to answer your own prayers.

YOU CAN GIVE - God has given you the privilege of being responsible for a portion of His money. Decide how much you can keep for yourself, then use the rest to further God's kingdom. One way is to support foreign mission work.

YOU CAN SEND - Look around in your church or community. Seek out another who senses a call to missions, then spur that person on and encourage them to further seek Gods direction for their life.

Adopt a missionary. Give him moral support. Encourage him through letters or tapes; let him know that you believe in him and in the work God has called him to. Maybe you are in the position to offer him a place to stay or a car to use while he's on home assignment.

YOU CAN GO - The great commission is a call to you too! You can see the need. Why delay?

Contact us if you want to know more.

OM Literature,
P.O. Box 1047, 129 Mobilization Drive
Waynesboro, GA 30830-2047, U.S.A.

U.S. CENTER FOR WORLD MISSION

How I thank God For the U.S. Center for Word Mission! This unique, wonderful enterprise insists on the primacy of reaching for Christ the world's unreached peoples in order to finish the Church's God-given task. The Global Prayer Digest it produces is a real force in grass roots education concerning peoples still without the Gospel. It's multi-faceted activities offer you an opportunity you should embrace to learn as you serve here with us what God's priorities for his people really are. Average lay people from a wide variety of backgrounds are finding fulfillment here at the USCWM. Why not you?

Norm Lewis

"You are welcome to the USCWM. We are 300 full time people, speaking forty languages, with backgrounds in 70 mission agencies, and fields in every part of the world. Come and visit, take the tour stay a while volunteer See where God might want you to go next. With over 100 departments we can easily use any skill or no skill experience or no experience. We try to serve mission agencies, local congregations, student groups, anyone seriously concerned about completing the Great Commission by the year 2000. We run our own university. You can work and study!"

Dr. Ralph Winter, Founder

William Carey International University
1539 E. Howard, Pasadena. CA 91104 (818) 797-1200

U.S. Center for World Mission
1605 E. Elizabeth, Pasadena. CA 91104 (818) 797-1111

THE EVANGELICAL ALLIANCE MISSION (TEAM)

For over fifty years, I have known and rejoiced in the vast work of The Evangelical Alliance Mission (TEAM). It is one of the largest, most reliable agencies in the world which exists for the purpose of evangelizing the world with the good news of Jesus Christ. In that task some 1000 missionaries now serve in 41 fields. Several practical avenues are open if you wish to explore possible service with TEAM.

Norm Lewis

"At TEAM we are committed to helping you find your place in this world. We have a staff whose passion is to explore what God may have for your life. TEAM exists for people who are radically committed to Christ and want to help establish a church for people who live in darkness. Your time commitment may be weeks, months, or years, but your commitment to the lost would be 'Priority One'. We are praying for those that are sold out for God and His purpose, who want to do something significant with their lives, and who are ready to do what it takes to see God's plan completed. We'd love to work with you and your church to help you on your way. Give us a call."

George Murray, General Director

PO. Box 969, Wheaton, IL. 60189-0969
1-800-343-3144
Bev@TEAMworld.org

Airways P.O. Box 56030
Calgary Alberta T2E 8K5
1-800-295-4160

ABOUT THE AUTHOR

Norm Lewis became a believer in 1934 as a premed student at the University of Nebraska. He graduated in 1938, then studied at St. Paul Bible Institute, Wheaton College, Northwestern University and Nyack Missionary Training College. He and his wife, Annabeth, were sent to Argentina by the Christian and Missionary Alliance in 1945, where their work became interdenominational with the beginning of La Voz, a Spanish evangelistic publication which grew to a circulation of 180,000 copies.

The Lewises returned to the United State in 1960 with their eight children and Norm became Mission Conference Director at Back to the Bible Broadcast. In 1963 he was appointed president of King's Garden, an evangelical conglomerate in Seattle, where he served five years, meanwhile earning his Ph. D. in history at the University of Washington. For two years, he taught at Whitworth College in Spokane, then joined the faculty of Western Conservative Baptist Seminary in Portland. In 1977, he began serving at the US Center for World Missions at Pasadena. Since 1983, the USCWM has loaned Norm to Frontiers, a new group focusing on witness to Muslims.

Mr. Lewis has authored a number of books including:

Go Means You
Bible Themes Memory Plan
Triumphant Missionary Ministry in the Local Church
Handbook: Faith Promise for World Witness
Success God's Way

Norm Lewis
P.O. Box 40159, 1610 Elizabeth St., Pasadena, CA 91104

Faith Promise

Why and How?

Norm Lewis

Edited by: Helena Boerchers

This powerful plan can help your chuch to:
Support missionaries;
Start churches;
Evangelize the world.

LITERATURE
P.O. Box 1047
Waynesboro, GA 30830 U.S.A.
ph (706)554-5827

This book if for:

- Pastors and church leaders,
- Missions committee members;
- Leaders of missions agencies;
- People interested in Faith Promise;
- Anyone helping a congregation understand Faith Promise;
- Whoever wants to increase giving to advance Christ's Kingdom.

CONTENTS

Foreword

A great many churches have been using the concept of Faith Promise for many years, but there has been very little written about it. I feel indebted to Norm Lewis for the work he has done in order to produce this book. I have been involved in world missions conferences at many churches and my experience would lead me to agree heartily with his statement, "Faith Promise produces far more money for missions than any other method."

My father, Oswald J. Smith, learned the Faith Promise system when he was pastor of the Christian and Missionary Alliance church in Toronto. It was the Alliance that developed the system, however, they used the word "pledge". Father had been a Presbyterian minister in a church that took pledges from its people to support the local work. On occasion they would remind the people that they still owed something on their pledges. They treated the pledge in the same manner as they treated the electric, phone, or gas bill.

Because of this unfortunate connotation of the word pledge my father looked for another way to express the same idea and he came up with the words Faith Promise. He introduced the Faith Promise system in hundreds of churches throughout the world. Norm Lewis worked shoulder to shoulder with my father for many years, and he learned this system of giving better than any other man I know. When I read the manuscript of this book in its early stages I wrote to him and said that I could easily believe this was written by my father. But my father went to be with the Lord before he had explained the system in any of his books.

Norm Lewis goes through the mechanics of how to make a Faith Promise offering in detail. Any pastor could read this book and then launch the Faith Promise system in his church without the help of anyone else. I would say most emphatically to my fellow pastors: Read this book, study this book, put the principles of this book into practice and the missionary work of your church will be revolutionized.

Thank you, Norm Lewis.

Dr. Paul B. Smith, Pastor
Peoples Church, Toronto

Introduction

The Faith Promise Plan is head and shoulders above other methods of financing the advance of God's Kingdom beyond current frontiers. Why? Above all else it offers a pastor a more effective means to motivate each person in his congregation to prayerfully consider his part.

The FP Plan is a tool aiding the Church to achieve its top priority. Faith Promise givers are funding gospel pioneers on Christianity's frontiers. They are supporting missionaries who are planting churches in people groups long neglected.

God has ordered Christians to evangelize everyone everywhere with the gospel of his Son. He puts that task first. To obey God is to focus on that. Life is a stewardship and we will reap what we sow. The FP Plan is a tool which enables believers to give more to sow the good seed of the gospel.

We must build on Jesus Christ, the only foundation, works that will stand God's test. His order is, "Go, make disciples of all nations" (Matt. 28:18). Many "good works" are less important than that. The good may be the enemy of the best. Flawed works will fail when tested by fire (1 Co. 3:9-15).

Those who obey will hear God say, "Well done," and receive rewards. The FP Plan is helping countless Christians who hunger to please God.

Chapter 1

What is a Faith Promise?

A Faith Promise is a voluntary commitment a person makes to give a fixed amount to a church's missions budget within a year. In order to determine the amount the giver is encouraged to pray. In turn the giver mature in godliness as he exercises faith to make the payments. FP responsibility is solemn because the promise is made primarily to God. No one is persistently asked for payment. The FP is between the giver and God.

I like the way Richard Cowser puts it: "A Faith Promise is an agreement we make with God. It is a promise because of the agreement to provide a certain amount over a specific period of time to missions. It requires faith because we are trusting God to provide these funds in various ways. It is personal because we surrender to Him what we have, in order that He will supply what is lacking. This agreement is made between God and us alone."

Benefits of the FP Plan are impressive. The pastor encourages each member in the congregation to fill out an FP card showing how much they will endeavor to give each week for a year for world evangelization. The total sum then becomes the missions budget for the coming year.

The great strength of FP lies in its harmony with the whole Word and work of God. It is not 'gimmicky'. It promotes heartily the faith which the Bible recommends. As the author of Hebrews affirms, "Without faith it is impossible to please God" (Heb. 11:6). Faith is essential for the believer. The Bible goes so far as to say that "everything that does not come from faith is sin" (Romans 14:23). "The righteous will live by faith" is God's way for all who follow Him (Romans 1:17).

The usual explosive increase of giving for missions when the FP Plan is launched will rapidly expand the potential for world outreach. The church will have far more funds for missionary work than ever before. Also as people learn to give for Christ's witness abroad, they give to the home work as well and thus all church finances are strengthened.

Recently I heard of the Shades Mountain Independent Church in Birmingham, Alabama. One evening at a meeting held in a basement of a home a missionary explained FP giving. That year they made a FP of $3,000 for missions. Today the church has FPs totaling more than $400,000 and share in the support of over 123 missionaries.

If the principles of the FP Plan had been less than solid, weaknesses would surely have surfaced long ago. Churches that have used the plan successfully for decades are evidence of its merit. In scores of churches practicing FP the pastor has led in establishing a pattern of missionary giving that increases consistently. God's redemptive purpose is as firm today as ever. He has commanded his Church to sustain missionaries until he sends his Son to earth again. Implement FP giving to increase long term support of God's worldwide purpose.

Consider another church that learned what FP giving is through the growth and blessing it brought. Donald A. Jensen, Pastor of the Village Baptist Church, in Beaverton, Oregon says, "Does it work? Of course Faith Promise giving works. Let me explain. In the New Testament a number of offerings are mentioned including the tithe, hospitality for itinerant workers, special needs, the widows mite, and what we call today a Faith Promise offering. This offering is called FP because a Christian in faith asks God to provide funds, and promises to give as God provides.

"In the Bible it was used to meet non-local needs. It is not a cash offering; it is a faith offering. The person promises to give what God provides in response to his faith. Paul illustrated this with a farmer sowing in faith believing that the sun and the rain God provided would prosper the seed he committed to the ground in order to permit him to reap.

"This offering is international in nature. The apostle Paul, a Jewish believer from Tarsus, wrote to the Corinthians in Greece, using the Macedonians as an example, and asked them to give what they had promised a year earlier for the sake of some poor Jews in Judea.

"Here at Village we began to trust God for these additional funds when our missionary offering was still part of the general budget. We were giving $14,500 toward missions and did not know where we could get more. We followed the apostle's pattern and asked God to provide through us $25,000. We cracked the $29,000 barrier and saw our general budget increase as well!

"Today our outreach has continued to multiply. This doesn't happen automatically. It works for those with a mind and heart to respond to needs. One-third of this planet's population has not yet heard the name of Jesus. Another third has heard enough about him to make a decision. We must do all that we can to relieve this terrible ignorance of the gospel.

"How will God provide? In ordinary ways and in special ways. One of his favorite ways to provide is through the discipline of lifestyle changes. On the local scene it begins

with the leaders. They are the ones to whom Paul wrote in
order that they might encourage the rest of their people to see
God work. Does it work? Of course! God is behind it!"

There is magnetism in concern for others. People are
drawn to churches that give unselfishly to meet needs worldwide. The people of Village Baptist Church have found the
secret of blessing. They are aiming for God's global goal,
knowing that Christ for all people is God's priority. FP giving
is authentic, biblical and Christ-honoring.

If a church is looking for the best way to implement
FP giving, here are two essentials:

1. **Hold an annual missions event.** Make this the most
significant happening on the church calendar. Plan it well.
Obtain qualified speakers. Teach the basic meaning of
missions. Build it on the Bible. Have missionaries present.
This is crucial for maximum spiritual impact.

2. **Set a missions goal each year.** A financial goal calls for
commitment. Many churches suffer from aimlessness. A
missionary event without a goal is pointless. The church can
be like a car with the motor running but going nowhere.
Sunday after Sunday the same routine unfolds but with no
goal. Set a missionary goal! People will be lifted and
challenged by it.

Enhance your church's corporate commitment to
Christ's work world wide by FP giving.

Chapter 2

Faith Promise Benefits

The church that starts Faith Promise will immediately benefit. Good results will be almost instant. Pastor Phil Spry writes, "Our missions giving went up nearly 300 percent after initiating FP in our newly planted church. Faith Promise works."

As Spry experienced, several benefits suddenly blossom when FP giving begins. Notice a few of those immediate local benefits:

The FP Plan heightens sensitivity to the Christian's accountability to God. The pastor explains a few weeks prior that FPs will be received. He asks his people to pray about their personal Faith Promise, reminding them that God owns everything and we are but his stewards. This becomes meaningful when a person asks himself, "How much will my weekly FP be?"

The FP Plan does not count on the churches general fund. Often missionary activities are financed from the church's general fund. The FP Plan sets up a separate mission budget and account. The fact that FP giving provides an important part of the support for one or more missionaries, is a powerful force to unite the congregation in a common cause. They know that missionaries serving in hard places, bonded to the congregation by a common commitment, count on their support. This holds the church together like glue.

The FP Plan exalts a common cause that serves to subordinate petty divisions. I recall a church that was on the verge of splitting because of internal wrangling. When emotions were high and permanent rupture seemed inevitable, an elder spoke. In a mature way he reminded the people that several loved missionaries would lose critical support if the church split. That consideration kept the congregation together.

How healthy is your congregation? This questions is difficult to answer. Hearty response to the FP Plan is both a cause and an evidence of spiritual vitality.

The FP Plan provides active involvement in an exercise that glorifies God. People who make a first time FP enter an exciting new chapter of their Christian experience. There is a sense of hands-on participation in providing for the advancing of God's Kingdom to new frontiers. Giving to promote the progress of God's worldwide purpose is meaningful.

FP giving furnishes content for a dynamic and encouraging public testimony. Unchurched people are impacted for good when they see Christians as generous people. Curiosity often prompts them to wonder why Christians would give largely for the well-being of unknown people in distant lands..

FP giving emphasizes living by faith in a way that becomes blessedly contagious. People who practice FP giving offer countless testimonies authenticating the intervention of God in their lives. Prayer is asking; answered prayer is receiving. Much of what the Bible teaches about prayer underlines that reality. The whole FP idea rests on interaction between the FP maker and God.

People who participate in the FP Plan tend to grow in the grace and knowledge of Christ. So often it is possible to share in evangelistic activities without exercising the "muscles of faith." Because of this people are surprised when encouraged to seek God prayerfully about the amount of their FP. As they do so in humble obedience, they become increasingly aware of their vital relation to God. Their grip on spiritual realities makes them more able to cope with life's hard challenges.

The FP Plan can be a solid factor in producing numerical church growth. There is something magnetic about the evidence of unselfish giving. It attracts people. Visitors are drawn to churches whose passion is sharing God's good news with unreached people is a clear priority.

A pastor who appreciates the values of these considerations will sense that a useful tool is offered in the FP Plan. It is never too soon for a church to launch the FP Plan. It will strengthen the church in many ways, the above are only a start.

Chapter 3

I Love Faith Promise

Why? Several reasons. Many churches experience an explosive increase in money for missions when they start Faith Promise giving. When a church launches the FP Plan it will commonly increase its missions giving one hundred percent in a year. Often the total will jump two or three-fold.

I have seen this occur with such regularity that I expect it to happen. Faith must not focus on the plan; that would be wrong. Jesus said, "Have faith in God" (Mark 11:22). Faith's sole focus must be God. Recognize that fact and God will respond. **Starting the FP Plan in a church usually means far more money for missions.**

FP giving avoids the problem caused by giving a percentage of the overall church income to missions. What problem? A church that gives a fixed part of its income to mission will find it very hard to increase that percentage. Why? The percentage for missions is a slice of the pie which supports all activities of the church. To increase that percentage means to take it away from other church programs. The congregation's perception that its leaders propose to "Rob Peter to pay Paul" is almost sure to provoke resistance. Hard feelings may follow. The larger the increase to missions, the more painful the ordeal to some people. The problem seems inherent in a unified budget.

A church should always be seeking to give more to missions. The desire should never cease. To increase the amount year after year ought to be an exhilarating experience. After all, world evangelization is God's idea (Mark 16:15-16). If people think the plan is to take money for missions from other programs it will not prosper.

FP giving goes to a separate budget. To put more into missions does not hurt the funding of other programs. Experience shows it will actually increase giving to local needs. This is a great advantage. The missions enthusiast can give as much as he wants to missions. The person less convinced can support local needs. Thus both are content. **FP giving does not regiment people. It promotes liberty and harmony.**

FP is linked with the most important work on the earth! That fact adds much to its value. From the time FP giving started it has been used primarily to support the work of world evangelization. God intends his Church to offer everyone on earth an opportunity to find life through His Son. The FP Plan has been a major factor in enlisting thousands of Christians to undergird that task. The relevance of the plan has thus widened and deepened to the present hour.

God's plan for world evangelization unites the Bible from Genesis to Revelation. Churches everywhere should use FP giving to help finish the task. **The prime use of FP giving from its birth to the present hour has been to support the world's most important work.**

FP giving for missions is not fund raising so much as a matter of the heart. It flows from an attitude of worship that offers back to God all he has given to us. When Christians are aware of people without Christ and are challenged from God's Word to make an FP, they respond. This giving brings rich inward rewards.

The Plan emphasizes that every person who desires to make an FP should seek God's guidance. No FP is to be dictated by the church or set by human standards. FP giving is based on the relation to God of people who have been saved by a great salvation. Gratitude, love and trust are its foundations.

Mary, the mother of Jesus, long ago pointed some perplexed servants to Christ and told them, "Whatever he says to you, do it!" In the same way, before any FPs are received, the wise pastor will point his congregation to Christ, who alone can confirm to each heart the amount of their individual FP.

Scores of people have told me how FP practice has brought them closer to God. It has increase their awareness that God is the one to whom they must give an account. They have proved that when God commands us to give, he also provides the resources to enable us to obey. Remember Moses' words, "but remember the Lord your God, for it is He who gives you the ability to produce wealth" (Deut. 8:18).

In these and other ways, **FP has moved countless people into a closer relationship to God through Jesus Christ.** It has helped create a new intimacy with him. If it deserved praise for nothing else, this would be a strong recommendation of its value. FP giving encourages godliness in the people who practice it.

The FP Plan teaches people to pray expectantly. True prayer is an essential part of the priesthood of the believer which is taught in the Bible. Prayer is two-way communication between God and the one who prays. God says, "Call unto me and I will answer you ... ask and it shall be given you, seek and you shall find ... if any of you lacks wisdom, he should ask God who gives generously ... and it will be given to him." Prayer is asking; answered prayer is receiving. **FP energizes and encourages prayer; it confirms confidence in God's faithfulness.**

These are reasons I love FP.

Chapter 4

Where it Started

Though the Faith Promise concept has been around a long time, it is not a patented idea. Confusions sometimes occurs because FP means different things to different people. Despite some diversity in its definition, FP in practice remains remarkably similar in many churches.

When I asked the late A.W. Tozer about its origin, he said, "Dr. A. B. Simpson (founder of the Christian and Missionary Alliance) used it in conferences at Old Orchard Beach, Maine during the last two decades of the 19th century. "Of course," Tozer added, "Simpson thought he got the plan from the Apostle Paul." Simpson was influenced by the Apostle Paul's inspired teaching in Second Corinthians 8 and 9. Calling this special kind of giving "Faith Promise", Simpson found a handle to help people greatly increase their missionary giving. Thus FP giving began on the U.S. East Coast a century ago.

What prompted Simpson to launch the FP Plan? His heart was burdened for the peoples of the world who had never heard God's offer of salvation through His Son, Jesus Christ. This burden almost consumed Simpson and strongly influenced his anointed career. He was a poet and songwriter. Here is one stanza of a hymn he wrote:

A hundred thousand souls a day
Are passing one by one away
In Christless guilt and gloom
Without one ray of hope or light
With future dark as endless night
They're passing to their doom.

How could Christians respond to such an awesome need? How could they contribute more in order to give unevangelized people the gospel? The FP Plan was Simpson's answer. FP sprang from a spiritual burden based on Christ's command to offer all people everywhere eternal life.

Paul Josephson writes, "I became involved in Faith Promise giving thirty years ago. A friend of mine moved to Indianapolis and joined a small church with a missions budget of $3,500. Soon the church began FP. I visited my friend year after year and saw his spiritual life grow markedly and in ten years saw the church increase its missions giving to over $100,000. As a result my own church began FP for missions." When a church has a vision for missions, it will grow. God blesses churches that make missions their priority. God is the great giver. He models the giving we must imitate. "For God so loved the world that He gave His one and only Son that whoever believes in Him shall not perish but have eternal life" (John 3:16). FP giving honors God through its harmony with the Bible's central thrust.

A critical factor with any plan is the caliber of the people who put it into operation. The most dynamic plan ever devised will remain dead apart from the people. The FP is no exception; its success depends primarily on the character of those who practice it.

Seen from every practical standpoint, the pastor is the

key to the Plan's success. He stands alone in his power to lift his people spiritually to a vantage point from which to survey earth's Christless masses. As Jesus said, "Open your eyes and look at the fields! They are ripe for harvest" (John 4:35).

The heaviest load is always on the person who leads. A true pastor must bear the burden of his lonely position. He must live out the commitment he expects of his people if the FP Plan is to prosper. Blessed is the church whose pastor inspires imitation along right lines. In prayer, planning and enthusiastic promotion, he must pay a large price. However his privileges are also great. God will always empower his Word when it is delivered in dependence on his grace and for his glory. The Spirit-filled pastor who promotes FP will see his church prosper. People of character, led by a godly pastor, are keys to success with the FP Plan.

Let's consider the example of a church that started FP giving years ago and has continued to reap its blessings. Grace Evangelical Church was a new church of some 90 adults meeting in rented facilities in suburban Atlanta, Georgia, when they called Bill Waldrop to be their pastor. At that point they were giving $3,000 a year to missions. The new pastor was convinced that even a small, new church like theirs was biblically responsible for world evangelization. Concern grows for the salvation of neglected peoples as the congregation grows in the grace of giving. That meant to him "the ends of the earth as well as our area." He knew the FP system of funding missions had helped many churches dramatically increase their missions giving. Through the initial effort, missions giving increased to $8,000 that year.

During the second year, FPs increased to $23,000 and rose each year. Why? Waldrop says, "First, leaders in the church encouraged such giving and tried to model it personally. As I observed American culture, I was deeply convicted in my own life by Paul's declaration that greed is idolatry (Eph. 5:5; Col. 3:5). I realized that the great American idol was money and material possessions. My wife and I began to give as never before in our lives. We realized that we must set the pace for our congregation.

"Second, I learned that some eighty percent of all the Christian wealth in the world was in North America. The haunting words of Jesus in Luke 12:48 gripped me. 'From everyone who has been given much, much will be demanded.' American Christians had been given much; we owed much to the world not yet reached. So I taught biblical principles of handling money and material possessions.

"Third, we educated our people about the needs of the world. Before long God was calling people from the congregation to serve as cross-cultural missionaries. Sending our own, of course, heightened the congregation's interest in world evangelization.

"Fourth, we clearly delineated between what was properly the local ministry of the congregation and what was missions. The operating budget, for which we took no pledges, included local outreach, and evangelism. Regular giving funded this portion. FPs, collected at the end of the missions conference, entirely funded the missions program. Our people saw that their obligation as individuals and as a congregation was global and not simply local. Our conviction became so strong that the congregation covenanted not to build until its aggregate missions giving had reached the cost of the first building. And God honored their priorities." FP giving will build and bless any church committed to biblical goals.

Grace Evangelical Church started FP giving in a modest way. Its people stayed with the Plan, and their success honors God. Countless churches have had a similar experience. Congregations that have implemented FP giving for missions with success consider world wide witness for Christ their permanent priority. Some are making a study of unreached peoples. Teams are being formed to penetrate people groups with no church. They are pacesetters for others who will follow. Modern FP was birthed by a man burdened for people; it will prosper when practiced by pastors and congregations of like passion.

Chapter 5

Superior When Simple

Keep the FP Plan simple.

Let FP stand on its own merit; do not tie it to other financial obligations. People frequently define FP by relating it to other things. For example, it may be said, "Your FP must be over and above your local offering." This statement is counter productive because it is apt to exclude those who are not regular givers from making an FP.

There are better ways to present FP. Point out that it would be wrong to take money earmarked for some other essential need and apply it to an FP. Let FP giving for world evangelization be weighed on its own worth.

Others insist that only funds from a special source can be used to pay an FP. It is argued that they must come from a patently supernatural source. To make payments from funds one has on hand is frowned upon as presumably showing no faith. Granted that the biblical definitionin Hebrews speaks of faith as "the evidence of things not seen" (Heb. 11:1). But we should be careful not to apply that text in a way its author never intended.

Suppose a person has money saved to buy a coat and draws on that money to make an FP payment in the confidence that God will supply money to buy the coat. Surely the confidence that God will supply the coat in some way is a demonstration of faith. Yet the source of the FP payment was money the person had. My point is that we must not box in God's gracious ways of working by definitions that are too narrow. Let FP funds be derived from any of countless legitimate sources that express confidence and trust in God.

Let FP be recognized as related to the world's most worthy work. The dignity of FP derives from its close connection with the Church's most vital task. As John R. Mott said at the dawn of the twentieth century, "Missions work is not simply a desirable thing for the Church to carry forward, but it is her chief and most important undertaking. It is the reason for the existence of the Church, and should be made a controlling purpose in the life of each of the members. Every Christian, therefore, should be intelligently informed concerning the principal work of the Church." FP is a useful tool for every believer who seeks to make world evangelization a controlling purpose in his life. Its emphasis God-ward is one of its greatest values.

Let the challenge of finding funds to fulfill an FP enhance the quality of one's communion with God. Remember you are to go to God for guidance for the amount of your FP. Once you know what He wants, hold firmly to it. As Moses wrote, "Whatever your lips utter you must be sure to do because you made your vow freely to the Lord your God with your own mouth" (Dt. 23:23). The Psalmist exhorted, "Make vows to the Lord your God and fulfill them" (Ps. 76:11). And King Solomon advised, "When you make a vow to God, do not delay to fulfill it. He has no pleasure in fools; fulfill your vow. It is better not to vow than to make a vow and not fulfill it" (Eccl. 5:4-5).

This is not to exclude in any sense the essential presence and work of God in fulfilling any FP. God will be faithful, yes, but so too must the person be who makes the FP. Balance between the human and the divine elements must be maintained in order to enjoy God's blessing. The utterances quoted above from some of history's greatest men remind us that an FP, though simple, is a solemn thing. Who can measure the full meaning of commitments made to God in prayer?

Churches that use the FP plan with success inspire their people to participate. To accomplish that, keep FP giving plain and positive. Assimilate the best aspects of the FP plan as applied in churches you admire. However, curb the impulses to innovate. To modify FP fundamentals is risky because of difficulties such changes often create. For many years I have observed FP giving and its results in many churches. The method holds huge potential for supporting world evangelization. Of course perils are always present.

There are persons who want to tinker with the Plan and alter it in one or more ways. The FP card is a frequent target of those who want to change things. A simple yet effective statement for the FP card follows:

> "In dependence upon God, I will endeavor to give $................. each week for the worldwide outreach of (name of church).
>   Signed: ....

Some folks believe they can do better. One wants to print 20 or 30 amounts from which the giver must choose. Another wants to fill the card with appropriate Scripture exhortation. I am not opposed to changes made for good reason, but changes like the above do not seem to improve FP giving. The one matter we must keep before the potential donor is the right decision as to the amount he will dare to trust God for each week.

Let simplicity and effectiveness be the hallmark of your FP Plan. Avoid adding features, which might limit its usefulness in your culture. Present the FP Plan as an essential part of our response to our Lord's command to make disciples in all the world.

The FP Plan, like the goose that laid the golden egg, can be killed. Any distraction affecting a person who is considering making an FP should be avoided. Make each meeting for receiving FP also a renewed invitation to personal commitment to God. Let FP giving encourage dependence on God for his glory alone.

Chapter 6

Faith Promise Honors God

I believe in the theological integrity of FP giving. It invites the application of those principles of faith taught and demonstrated in the Bible. The FP Plan does not involve fanaticism or gimmickry. It is not a lottery which claims divine endorsement. Nor does it presume to unlock a deposit of some special sort of new faith. FP appeals only to that faith described in the Bible from Genesis to Revelation.

It should surprise no one to be told that faith is not an option for the believer. It is a basic requirement from the moment God begins to draw a person to Himself. Jesus said, "No man can come to Me unless My Father draws him." Faith is a part of that mysterious transaction by which a person becomes a new creation in Christ Jesus. God is so insistent that his people live by faith that in the New Testaments it is written that "Without faith it is impossible to please Him (God)" (Heb. 11:6). The Apostle Paul categorically declares, "Whatsoever is not of faith is sin" (Rms. 14:23). The FP Plan encourages use of the faith the Bible exalts.

A pastor who did much during his lifetime to encourage the wide use of the FP Plan, first experienced the blessing of FP giving in the early 1930's during the heart of the Great Depression. At that time many people did not have one dollar to rub against another. They were encouraged to trust God for FP funds for which the source was entirely unknown. That was all that most of them could do because of the hard times. They trusted and were greatly blessed in proving the faithfulness of God.

Today the situation is very different. Countless thousands of Christians are well-to-do. They own homes, cottages, lake properties, cars, boats, bank accounts, stocks, bonds, computers, electronic equipment - the list is endless. Today, materialism is among the deadly enemies Christians face, particularly in the Western world.

Some may argue that more faith is required to trust God for money from an unknown source. Perhaps. But does that mean the person who has something and gives it to God shall by definition be said to be without faith? Surely, such a judgment would be wrong. We should give to God because we love and trust him and have confidence in his integrity. Actions that stem from those convictions express faith. FP giving encourages the exercise of faith which embraces one's person and possessions - everything!

The most complete Bible presentation of FP principles is found in Second Corinthians, chapter 8 and 9. Note the essence of giving emphasized there.

1. A need was anticipated before it became a pressing problem (2 Cor. 8:6, 10, 11; 9:2).
2. The amount was specific enough to need to be paid in full and to be mentioned as a model to others (8:6,11; 9:2).
3. The FP commitment was made joyfully and without compulsion (8:2; 9:7).
4. With God's enabling they gave by faith "as much as they were able and even beyond their ability" (8:3).
5. God was the unfailing source of supply, much beyond their ability (9:8-11).

6. Believers were challenged and encouraged to do more
   by faith than they normally would. Paul vigorously
   exhorted them to act, and sent Titus and others to do the
   same (8:1-6, 16, 18, 24).
7. They were asked to put money apart every week for the
   purpose (1 Cor 16:2).
8. "They gave themselves first to the Lord" (2 Cor. 8:5),
   then to serve Paul's missionary band.

Pastors who lead their people into that attitude of faith
find blessing. Clifford Clark, when pastor of Tulsa Baptist
Temple, wrote me saying, "We have over 100 young people
in full-time service for Christ, 26 of them on foreign mission
fields. That never would have happened if we had not started
the FP Plan for missionary support years ago." Churches that
practice FP giving experience remarkably similar results.

The late Dr. G. Christian Weiss, missionary with Back
to the Bible Broadcast, learned how one church answered the
truths of God's love and humanity's lostness. He was invited
to speak at the Peoples Church in Toronto, Canada. Weiss
says, "Inevitably I was impressed by the missionary outreach
of the church and by the large sums of money given to foreign
missionary work. But it was not until I was invited back
several successive years that I began to ask myself, how is this
done?

"Why does this particular church give so much money
to foreign missions? Why are other churches not matching the
pattern? Was the church exceptionally rich? Was the bulk of
this missionary money given by a few very wealthy people?
Was it given by outsiders who chose to channel their missionary money through the Peoples Church because of its
nondenominational character? Were the large sums of money

merely commensurate with the size of the church?

"To each of these possible explanations the answer was in the negative. I knew the church well enough to know this. Finally it boiled down in my own mind to this: Could it be the particular program and method used in the church? Well, what was their method? What was the program they followed? That answer was easy to find - a strong annual missionary convention for presenting the appeal and challenge of missions to the people, and FP giving.

"To verify my thinking I then asked, are other churches using a similar method? If so, what are the results? I began noting various churches and the programs they followed. The result convinced me that an annual missionary conference and FP giving are essential in the program of any local church."

FP giving in innumerable churches honors God in its motive, method and results.

Chapter 7

Adopting Faith Promise

God's Word declares undeniably that his purpose through the Church is to evangelize the world. God's plan is logical. All people have sinned and face a lost eternity. Thus we must make every effort to offer to all, God's one way to salvation through Christ's death and resurrection.

FP is an excellent means to help the Church do that work. God's aim to evangelize the world was revealed to Abraham, Isaac and Jacob (Gen. 12:3; 26:4; 28:14). God promised Abraham that all people on earth would be blessed through him. Some two thousand years later, Jesus spoke of that promise saying, "Your father Abraham rejoiced to see my day: and he saw it, and was glad" (John 8:56). The Holy Spirit made the matter even more clear through the Apostle Paul. He said, "The Scripture foresaw that God would justify the Gentiles by faith and announced the gospel in advance to Abraham: 'All nations will be blessed through you'" (Gal. 3:8).

God's redemptive purpose spans the entire Bible. The Israelites were asked to treat foreigners well "so that all the peoples of the earth may know your name and fear you" (2 Chr. 6:33). The psalmist prayed, "That your ways may be known on earth, your salvation among the nations" (Ps. 67:2). Again, "Declare his glory among the nations, his marvelous deeds among all peoples" (Ps. 96:3). Isaiah sounded the theme as he told of God's Servant who would, "bring justice to the

32

nations" (Is. 42:1). He added God's further promise, "I will also make you a light for the Gentiles, that you may bring my salvation to the ends of the earth" (Is 49:6).

Encourage your church to embrace fully God's global goal as the motivation for the FP giving. Every congregation should share in achieving worldwide witness for Christ. FP implements reaching that objective.

Seek an early church decision to adopt the FP Plan. Once the church starts talking of whether or not to use the FP Plan, set a date by which the decision will be made. Show your people that FP giving is simple and will advance the church's goals.

Help your church to view FP in simple terms. Persuade gently. If objections are raised, seek opportunities to pacify and persuade. Opposition to change is normal in churches. Be wise; be tactful. Find common ground and avoid arguments. Press forward patiently, persistently, knowing that FP will be good for your church.

Move to full dependence on the FP Plan in a single step. Plan to shift total support of your missions program to FP in a single step. That is better than trying to combine an old procedure with a new one. Do not split support between the old system and FP. That would cause confusion and put your FP effort at risk. Explain the change in advance. Illustrate with specific examples. Suppose the church has been giving 10% of its income to missions. Before you start FP, show with a bulletin insert how a person can give the same to missions through FP as he gave before, or more if he wishes.

Does it seem risky to base all mission support on FP alone? Experience shows that when FP is explained well, the change is practical and positive in its results. The secret is to make clear to each giver what he must do by FP to equal or improve what he did before.

Plan an annual missions conference with an effective speaker. An annual missions event to emphasize the importance of world evangelization is an essential element of the FP Plan. Make this an effort "of the whole church, by the whole church, and for the whole church." During this time set aside or re-schedule other activities. Do not let competition dilute the church's focus on world evangelization.

Invite the best available speaker a year in advance. He must be able to expound effectively the Biblical basis of missions. If the church is changing to the FP Plan, a speaker should be chosen whose track record proves him qualified. The speaker may be the hinge on which your success hangs.

Build the budget on the main issue: offering life eternal to people dead in sin. Support world evangelization as Christ defined it. He showed the awesome consequences of the task when he said, "He who believes and is baptized will be saved. He who does not believe will be damned" (Mark 16:15-16). Christ made knowing and receiving him a matter of life and death. Support people and projects focusing on that supreme issue.

To include merely nice matters in the budget will diminish its importance as a channel that merits sacrificial giving. When missions is made to include all sorts of good causes, its life or death character is clouded. The whole reason to give everyone God's good news then falls to a lower level.

World evangelization means to give everyone on the earth a reasonable chance to receive Christ. It would seem that at least half of the church's giving should go for that purpose. (See Romans 10:14-15.) If an average of even one church in a hundred in the USA would plant a church in a people group which has none, all could soon hear. To reach that goal more churches must target unreached people, still without hope of eternal life.

Consider Paul's purpose in Romans 15:20-21. Paul made it the constant pursuit of his ministry "to preach the gospel where Christ was not known." If that was a compelling passion in the dawn of the Christian era, how much more it should fire our hearts and focus our plans in the final years of this century.

As one pastor puts it, "One of the healthiest things that can happen in your church is when people learn you are serious about being good stewards of resources designated to missions. Give to projects that merit support. Do the groundwork on all proposals in order to make responsible decisions."

Once the missions committee has determined the workers and projects that will benefit from the budget, promote it widely. Publicize it early, clearly, specifically. Give people substance for serious prayer about their FP.

People need time before FPs are received to decide what God would have them do. Strangely, this obvious need is often overlooked. The budget should be presented a month before your annual missions event.

Develop tools that will increase the value of the annual missions conference. Follow the example of churches that use a response form for gathering information. The First Baptist Church, Wichita, Kansas uses a response form. During a recent annual missions event they gathered the following valuable facts:

The FP total was $210,000 with 186 family units participating of which 40 were first-time commitments. There were 147 who promised to pray and/or correspond regularly with missionaries, 40 who were willing to consider short-term service, and 17 willing to consider long-term, cross-cultural ministry. Such data received each year is useful to measure spiritual vitality and aid in follow-up. (See sample response form in Chapter 10.)

Plan your FP card and church offering envelope as tools to increase the effectiveness of the FP Plan. They are vehicles for a message that should move people toward a meaningful goal. Don't trivialize their potential. Maximize their usefulness to influence people.

Emphasize either the amount needed each week or the total for the year as your missions financial goal. Consider carefully how you want people to think about how much they will give. Should they ask God how much they should give to missions for a whole year? Should they focus on how much they might give each week? There is a difference. In my early years receiving FPs we always projected the weekly sum on each card to get an annual amount to announce. Our emphasis was on the total amount for the year. More recently, we began presenting the weekly amount. People can focus more sharply on an amount they can trust God for each week rather than what may seem a huge total for the year. One advantage in emphasizing the weekly cycle is that Chrisitans can be shown how the amount they spend for ordinary things each week compares to their FP giving for world evangelization.

You need to choose to emphaise one or the other because your choice will affect the wording of the budget presentation, the thermometer, and related publicity.

Mold the Sunday School into an effective element in FP giving. Children can be taught to make meaningful FPs. They are well able to understand why the gospel must be given to everyone everywhere. Even the young can be helped by their teachers to make and fulfill FPs. Children will be a vital part of FP giving if you offer them the opportunity. Right training is an indispensable foundation.

Teach believers that they are God's stewards, overseeing his property to accomplish his purposes. Money matters are hardly mentioned by many pastors. They fear people will be offended. True, finances may be scary. To ignore them is wrong, yet tactless treatment will offend. What to do? God's whole counsel makes us accountable to him for assets we call ours, but really only hold for him. Jesus' parables and teachings are filled with references to finances.

When Christians begin to understand that they are not owners, but stewards entrusted with the management of God's property, the springs of giving start to flow. Agreement with God in this area may produce results nothing short of revolutionary. When that occurs, FP consequences count mightily for God.

Apply this teaching to major projects and programs in which missionaries of the church are involved. To build vital links with exciting projects overseas has potential for building vision in the congregation. "Lift up your eyes." Embrace God's global effort. Identify deeply with God's purpose to save sinners worldwide.

Present the making of FPs as a major act of personal and corporate commitment. Move with care toward the time for taking FPs. Treat the receiving of FPs as the high point of a climactic conference. Foster interest and expectation to a good goal. The making of the FP is both the commencement and the culmination of one's deliberate commitment to Christ. It should be viewed, however, as more than a personal act.

An FP for world evangelization is not merely a decision made by an individual. Nor could it be done as effectively apart from the church. It stems from the purpose of groups which constitutes locally the body of Christ. The FP goal expresses the church's corporate annual commitment to the cause dearest to God's heart. The group does it together, seeking God's guidance.

All FPs should be made during the annual missions event, not later. FPs that dribble in after the close of the event diminish that effort. To evangelize the world must always be the Church's central thrust. But to seek more money by letting people decide late is like the man who cut off his dog's tail a little at a time so it would not hurt so much. People can reasonably be asked to decide their FP and hand in the card before the conference closes.

Emphasize world evangelization as the church's permanent priority. Afterward, keep the world evangelization profile high. Plan creatively to keep attention focused on the church's main task. See that the global task is preached. Keep missions in view in other ways.

* Do a missions bulletin monthly or quarterly.
* Present missionary news in the bulletin or as an insert.
* Offer a 3-6 minute missionary update on Sunday mornings.
* Provide specific missionary information to the pastor to include in his Sunday morning prayer.
* Plan a monthly Sunday School missions emphasis.
* Have a Sunday School missions rally for adults once a quarter.

As a regular bi-monthly bulletin feature, inform the congregation how income for worldwide outreach is doing. This can be done by using a simple, easy-to-read format. (See illustration in chapter 10.) One secret of healthy finances is to advise people promptly of any shortage. Do it while the shortage is still small and can be corrected. Report "Over" with praise, or "Short" with appropriate exhortation.

What an honor, to offer God's gift of eternal life to all humanity! "How beautiful on the mountains are the feet of those who bring glad tidings of good things" (Rom. 10:15). The Bible shows giving as part of a seven-day cycle (1 Cor. 16:2). Secular society also follows that time pattern in ordering its affairs. This is not to insist that people make FP payments each week if they are being paid bi-monthly, monthly, or with some other frequency. Those who see weekly giving as meerly cultural, tend to believe the Lord's day and the giving normally included in it, are part of God's plan for his people. Certainly let us pray each week for the completion of God's redemptive plan worldwide. Prayer for that cause is praise-worthy.

Chapter 8

Picture Faith Promise Applied

I read of a man in Seattle who had long wanted a boat. He had set his heart on a cabin cruiser. He got a picture of the boat and put it where he could see it every day. What was the result? His dream came true; he got his cruiser. "Faith is the substance of things hoped for, the evidence of things not seen" (Heb.11:6). See your church as a part of God's plan for the world aided by the use of the FP Plan. Frame that vision like a picture. Fill in the details as you pray.

Ability to see goals in your mind will help you achieve them. A student at Amherst College put a large letter "V" over the door of his room. Friends asked what it meant, but he would not tell. Their curiosity turned to frustration, then to ridicule. The student shrugged off the ridicule and kept his secret. Four years later he graduated and was chosen to give the class valedictory oration. At last his friends understood. The mysterious "V" stood for valedictorian. It reminded the student of his goal through all his college years. He kept it before his minds eye until he achieved it. Do as he did in your purpose to please the Lord with the FP Plan

Christ focused on fulfilling God's purpose throughout his earthly ministry. After his resurrection, his one theme was God's world plan. "He openned their minds so that they could understand the Scriptures. He told them, 'This is what is written: That Christ will suffer and rise from the dead on the third day, and repentance and forgiveness of sins will be preached in his name to all nations" (Luke 24:45-47).

Christ linked his personal integrity to the Church's completion of world evangelization. He declared, "This gospel of the kingdom will be preached in the whole world as a testimony to all nations and then the end will come" (Matt 24:14). Picture the FP Plan aiding your congregation to support God's global goals.

Florence Chadwick was the first woman to swim the English Channel in both directions. She determined to be the first woman to swim the twenty-one miles from Catalina Island to the coast of California. She kept at it for fifteen hours through bone-chilling cold, through growing fatigue, and fog so dense it kept her from seeing even the boats beside her. She finally gave up and was lifted into one of the boats. Then she learned the shore was only a half mile away, though hidden by the fog. She said, "If I could have seen the shore, I might have made it." It was not the cold or even the fatigue that defeated her, but the fog which hid the goal. Keep your goal ever before you so when the fog comes you can carry on because you know that your goal is out there where it has always been. Circumstances hide it, however, it has not changed.

Chapter 9

Plan Well, It Pays

An annual missions conference is an effective means to explain and exalt redemption for all people, the Bible's theme from Genesis to Revelation. God asks us to do our part to evangelize the world while we trust him to do his. As we do what we can, God will do what we cannot. Without him we cannot; without us he will not. So work hard to get ready for the annual missions conference. Good preparation pays.

Faith asks us to accept God's plan, not our own. I was brought to Christ through the evangelistic efforts of a small Christian and Missionary Alliance church. Many capable missionaries came our way. They soon convinced me God's plan was to evangelize the world. Did I offer to be involved? Sadly, I did not. I had my own plans for my life and wanted God to approve them. The Holy Spirit convicted me of stubborn selfishness. A battle began. At last I surrendered to God and agreed to serve him anywhere he wanted me. That got me on track again.

God's highest purpose in world evangelization is the vindication of his own righteousness. That has been true from the dawn of God's dealing with our race. God knew his prophets would be heeded by few, yet he sent them. In our day he commands believers to offer salvation to all people whether they will hear of refuse. Either way, God's righteousness will be vindicated.

Faith Promise is valuable to the degree that it affords

vital support to God's redemptive purpose. Every pastor should place top priority on zealous preparation for the annual FP missions event. The Church must own God's world-embracing plan. Hands-on participation is what God wants from every person. Employ the FP Plan to aid you congregation to embrace God's goals worldwide.

My friend Tim Owen, of Ellensburg, Washington, knows the value of good preparation. He says, "As a pastor, I've watched our congregation of about 450 increase its annual giving from $20,000 to $98,000 in 5 years. I'm convinced that giving to missions is directly proportional to the level of importance and quality that the church places on missions."

Owen goes on to describe how he learned that lesson in 1984 when his church embarked on its largest one-time project ever, the building of a Christian Education annex. They employed a fund-raising organization and paid a consultant $15,000 before getting in even the first dollar in contributions. Owen explains the elaborate preparations, time and hard work which went into the effort. He adds, "God used the campaign to raise the money and today our building is complete and paid for.

"Such a successful campaign proved that our congregation could raise funds for what we wanted. Why, I wondered, was our giving to mission relatively small? Then I began to compare the energy we put into other projects, such as the building. By comparison, we grossly neglected missions." Owen tells of their traditional approach to the missions conference and adds, "With such a small measly effort, we were saying to people that missions wasn't that important.

"That next year our governing board and missions

committee decided to use the same method of developing awareness, commitment, and participation for missions as we did for the building. We established measurable goals to accomplish; to increase our Faith Promise from $20,000 to $75,000; to increase pledgers from 50 to 100; to recruit a year-round missions prayer team, a missionaries' support team, and 15 persons who would pursue God's call to cross-cultural missionary service.

"We recruited a Missions Conference Steering Committee and sent out teams to visit each household to build prayer support. We gave the entire month before the Conference to missions sermons, testimonies, decorations, and newsletters. We produced a 12 page brochure on our Conference and mission Program. When people received this in the mail, their eyes widened. 'What's going on this year in missions? Why the big deal? Is something important happening?' We successfully communicated that missions is important.

"We have now elevated mission education and promotion to the place of high priority it deserves. I believe that the prayer, funds, effort and quality the church invest in mission education and promotion are indicative of its prioritization of and passion for world evangelization. Our people respond accordingly, through personal involvement and financial giving."

Let us assume your church has agreed to launch the FP Plan at your first annual missions conference three months from now. Prepare six bulletin inserts, each describing a basic feature of the FP Plan in a simple way. Start six weeks before the mission event and release one of the inserts each Sunday.

Shift wholly to the FP Plan in one smooth step. Avoid the temptation to continue partial support of missions by the

previous method. Plan to take FPs and to receive the first
payment on them without delay. Do not make givers wait (as
some churches have tried) until the start of the church fiscal
year or some other future date. Invite FP payments as soon as
the missions meetings close.

Encourage all your people to give regularly to
missions by printing that option on the offering envelope. Print
a 'Missions/Faith Promise' option on the offering envelope
(illustrated in chapter 10) and make clear that it will be the
sole channel for supporting missions. The words 'Missions/
Faith Promise' on the envelope invites help from all people,
including those who did not make an FP. From time to time
remind the congregation that all Christians should invest in
world evangelization. Invite everyone to give regularly to
missions just as you would if the FP Plan did not exist. To do
so promotes unity.

Confirm dates for the annual missions conference and
speaker(s) a year ahead. Choose carefully the best speaker(s)
to lead your FP conference. A few suggestions follow:
* Write to Advancing Churches in Missions Commitment
  (ACMC), P.O. Box 3929, Peachtree City, GA, 30269-7929
  or phone 1-800-747-7346.
* Contact missionary sending agencies for names of men skilled
  in presenting the Biblical basis for missions and the FP Plan.
* Scan evangelical publications for authors of vital missions
  articles or information on mission leaders.
* Phone the speaker whom you favor and explain exactly what
  you want. If a man seems qualified, send him a copy of this
  book. You might invite him to speak at you church before
  deciding to have him for your conference. Or you might go
  to hear him speak elsewhere. Make sure he agrees with your
  church on major matter of the FP Plan. Take pains to let any

proposed speaker know your congregation's goals and
philosophy.

Finalize your missions budget at least a month before
your conference. Test each budget item by asking how it
relates to Christ's concern for the salvation of souls least-
reached. In many churches the missions budget has come to
include non-essential causes. Mold it gradually to focus on
offering life in Christ to people in cultures that have no church.
Direct budget strength to missionaries intent on pioneer, cross
cultural church planting. Support agencies and workers who
are committed to evangelizing peoples beyond Christianity's
frontiers.

Give such considerations practical value in choosing
missionary candidates. They need hands-on training in soul
winning and making disciples. Select workers to support
abroad as carefully as you would choose a pastor. Pick
winners. Invite them to your annual mission conference. The
impact of dedicated lives is enormous.

Put the missions budget in simple form on a large poster
at the front of the church. Print it in the church bulletin . The
last month before the conference have the pastor give facts on
budget objectives to fuel prayer about FPs.

Set up a goal oriented missions administration. Define
the role of the church mission committee realistically. It should
develop mission policies, review and update them as
necessary, and give broad oversight to missionary administration. The funds it manages belong in a separate bank account.
It should constantly watch over the church's missionary thrust
to see that its principle aim is to offer salvation through Jesus
Christ beyond present Christian frontiers.

If church strength permits, the committee should seek
an able missions administrator, ideally a capable person of

vision. Make that person responsible for mission administration according to the basis of the position description prepared by the elders and mission committee.

Use missionary music to press home truth which will transform people. Choose songs and choruses which impart world vision. Cause music to impact people with the importance of God's global goals. Do these things in a true spirit of worship. Let worship and obedience result in hands-on commitment to Christ's world cause in terms of Romans 12:1-2. Remind the music staff that all their art must communicate preeminently God's heart for the world's redemption and Christians' responsibility to "Go, make disciples."

The Sunday School can train world Christians for the next generation. I was in a missionary conference when a phone call came from a distant city. The caller made an FP of $15,000 for the church's missions budget. When asked what prompted his commitment, he said he had been taught as a boy in that church's Sunday School to make an FP every year. Encourage Sunday School classes to choose a missionary or couple from those the church supports to make their own in special ways. The class can get pictures of their missionary, remember birthdays, send holiday greetings, and develop other links.

Always contact parents in advance in order to win their understanding and good will regarding having their children participate in FPs. In younger children's classes have one FP for the class. If some want to make FPs, pool receipts in the class and turn in the total. Encourage older children to make individual FPs in their classes. When the FP is received, the SS superintendent is responsible to see that the number of FPs and their totals are reported immediately to the pastor to be announced in the congregational meeting.

Emphasize that the believer owns nothing; he is a steward who manages God's property. Commitment becomes effective to the degree that it impacts the congregations finances. We must often remind ourselves that we are not our own for we have been bought with a price. Our highest privilege is to be love slaves for Jesus. We are his servants, neither less nor more than that. How plainly Jesus put the matter. He said, "Suppose one of you had a servant plowing or looking after the sheep. Would he say to the servant when he comes in from the field, 'Come along now and sit down and eat'? Would he not rather say, 'Prepare my supper, get yourself ready and wait on me while I eat and drink; after that you may eat and drink'? Would he thank the servant because he did what he was told to do? So you also, when you have done everything you were told to do, should say, 'We are unworthy servants; we have only done our duty' (Luke 17:7-10). It is not easy to escape the conviction that world evangelization is our duty. As God's stewards, we must administer his assets in order to complete that work.

Plan the meeting in which FPs are to be received as high points in the annual church calendar. Build toward those meetings as times of major personal and corporate church commitment. Because faith without works is dead, and the Bible teaches that we must offer Christ worldwide, it is logical to make FPs.

Teach the congregation that the meetings to receive FPs will focus primarily on that act. It is one of the most unselfish kinds of giving a Christian can do. Plan one-fourth of the meeting time for pre-message elements, one-half for the message, and the last fourth for receiving FPs. Make this earnest act of the church, as a body, an experience to stretch each person's faith with a desire to play a larger part in world-wide witness for Christ. FP is a thrust of the whole church. It is best to shut the window for receiving FPs when the conference closes.

If people are allowed to make FPs later at will, many will not! Discourage late FPs. They are a concession to indecision and weaken the united effort of the church as a body. During the Missions conference the church has agreed together to trust God for a large amount for missions. Each person should make his FP as part of the group act.

Take special pains to prepare the program well for the days when FPs are to be received. Rehearse unusual procedures. The must by understood by all participants.

Urge Christians to keep the church aflame with passion for worldwide outreach. The active promotion of the pastor is most important in this matter. Like pastor, like people. No problem on earth outweighs the sin question and the urgent need to evangelize all peoples. The crucified, risen Christ is God's answer. Even emphasis on a missions budget is not enough. Church leaders must constantly address the issue of life and death. Few pastors make plain enough the prime need to give the gospel to everyone everywhere.

Make world vision the hallmark of your church. Ask yourself, "If I were a visitor to this church, would something here cause me to make an FP?" Remember, God loves the hundreds of ethnic groups still unreached by the gospel and Christ died for them.

The Apostle Paul said, "Now our salvation is nearer than when we first believed." The Bible links the Church's goal of finishing our global task with Christ coming again. To "Plan Well" for your churches annual missions conference is to plan for those events as well. Hold high world evangelization as the church's hallmark honoring Jesus Christ.

Chapter 10

Build Better Tools

Basic elements will improve or impoverish your conference. Make a list of tools you will need. Start early; build them right.!

Sell the budget with true enthusiasm. Give its main thrust the needed content to justify sacrificial FPs. To merely present dollar amounts does not motivate. Financial facts tend to have negative impact. Make your missions budget fit Jesus' definition of the work: to offer eternal life to people dead in sin.

In many churches the missions label covers too wide a variety of causes. Some may not really fit Jesus' order to his followers: "Go into all the world and preach the good news to all creation. Whoever believes and is baptized will be saved. But whoever does not believe will be condemned" (Mark 6:15-16). To mold the budget to meet humanity's most urgent need is worth constant, sustained effort. And God greatly blesses such obedience.

Dramatize the missions budget orally and visually prior to your missions event. Present the budget in simple form in the bulletin and display it on a platform poster. Make the poster large enough to be read from the rear of the auditorium. Use at least the space afforded by a four-by-eight foot plywood sheet. Explain the budget several times during the month before your annual FP event. Emphasize the need for every believer to seek God in prayer for guidance about his FP. Give budget facts in time for people to pray about meeting them.

A large platform poster will underline the importance of your world outreach effort.

MISSION BUDGET (Year)		
Carl and Betty Smith	$10,000	
Joe and Elsie Brown	14,000	
Bill and Eva Turner	12,000	
Literature	6,000	
Contingencies	3,000	
Current Giving		$ 45,000
PROPOSED INCREASE		
Smith increase	$ 3,000	
Sama and Eunice Graham	10,000	
		$ 13,000
GOAL		$ 58,000

Figure 1

Make and display a huge thermometer to dramatize your FP missions goal. Build a thermometer the same size as your budget poster. Construct a functional red center column. Cut a horizontal slot at the base of the column and a second one high enough to permit the red column to rise above the goal mark. Sew end to end two bands of cloth, one red and one white, each as long as the distance between the slots. Loop cloth through the slots, take up the slack, and sew the free ends together. The thermometer dramatizes the church FP goal. Paint dollar figures on the thermometer, as illustrated, with the goal near the top. But leave space above the goal to use in case FPs "break the thermometer." Place both posters at the front of the auditorium for high visibility.

Figure 2

Use wall poster, banners and displays featuring appropriate Bible text and world evangelization slogans. Encourage right thinking with statements like:

* I am debtor to give everyone the hope the gospel has given me.
* Give as you would want others to give if your family were part of an unreached people group.
* Christ promises that giving will govern rewards (Luke 6:38).
* It is as necessary for people to hear the gospel as it was for Christ to die.
* Dare we withhold from half the world the best news ever heard?
* A giving church is a living church.
* You would believe in pioneer missions if you were part of a people still unreached.
* Obey! Apathy will be punished. Obedience will be blessed.
* Church planting is like a bank, the more you put in the

more your interest grows.
* Not what we get but what we give, marks the worth of life we live.
* "Expect great things from God, attempt great things for God."   - *William Carey*
* "No reserve. No retreat. No regrets."
        -Bordon of Yale, died age 25 en route to the mission field.
* Give according to your income, lest God makes your income like your giving.

Arrest the attention of people who enter your auditorium with texts and slogans like these emphasizing the Church's God-given task. Initial impressions are important. Plan the church bulletin to reinforce that impact.

In your advertising, seek synonyms for 'missions' and 'missionaries' for those words have long had a poor press. Avoid clichés and negative stereotypes. Communicate with words to arouse interest and enlist cooperation. Create expectation. Charles Schwab, famous motivator of men in industry, said, "A man can succeed at almost anything for which he has unlimited enthusiasm." Present FP that way.

Demonstrate in every way you can that your church is different. Make world vision your hallmark. People are drawn to churches characterized by unselfish purposes.

Make your FP card a simple, one track tool. Keep the copy of your FP card and offering envelopes sparse and direct. Why complicate the card with a tear-off tab? Why make the giver choose an amount to give from a list of figures? Make the card simple (see Figure 4).

Send the card to everyone on your mailing list with a letter encouraging people to make an FP. Focus prayer on the meetings in which FPs will be received.

My Faith Promise to Share Christ Worldwide

In dependence on God, I will endeavor to give $.....................
each week for Grace Church's global gospel outreach.
Mark 16:15-16.

_____
(Name)

_____
(Address)

_____
(City)   (State)   (Zip)

Write in the space above the amount you purpose to give each week for
one year to share Christ worldwide. You will not be asked for payment; it
is a voluntary offering to God. Instructions for making payment will be
sent by mail.

Figure 3

Honor the weekly cycle of giving set by the Bible, but
allow people liberty to give with whatever frequency suits them
best. Tell donors they are free to make FP payments at any
time. Weekly giving is a good biblical norm.

Print a large, sparsely worded, user-friendly offering
envelope. Have envelopes printed as illustrated. Place
envelops in seat-back holders, on tables at rear of auditorium,
etc.

MY OFFERING
for
Grace Church

General Fund $_____
Missions - Check ( ) if Faith Promise $_____
Other $_____
                              Total $_____

Name or Number _____ Date _____

Figure 4

Prepare a response form to use in meetings toward the close of your conference. This will get your information for follow-up. Make the form brief and user-friendly. Distribute the response form and explain its purpose in at least two meetings.

MISSIONS CONFERENCE RESPONSE FORM
(Answer questions you feel apply to you.)

1. Which word best describes your interest in this missions event? (Circle one) **Intense**   **Good**   **Average**   **Poor**
2. How could we make our next conference more to your liking?
3. What missionary would you like to know better and why?
4. Would you like an opportunity for short-term service? Explain.
5. Would you consider full-time, cross-cultural ministry? Explain.
6. Have you ever made a Faith Promise for missions?
7. How do you feel about making an Faith Promise now?

Name: _____ Phone: _____
Address: _____
City: _____ State: _____ Zip: _____
We invite you to sign. Information will be kept confidential.
Thank you.

Figure 5

Receiving FPs is a spiritual exercise. Verify results and announce the FP total before dismissing the congregation. Make the announcing of the FP total the climax of the meeting.

Prepare in advance the follow-up letter showing appreciation to send to every person who makes an FP. Have it ready to send the day after FPs have been received. You might say:

Dear Donor:

Thank you for your Faith Promise to help us share Jesus Christ worldwide. God has commanded us to "go everywhere in the world and preach the good news to the whole world." Results for eternity hinge on our obedience.

Use an offering envelope like the one enclosed when making payments on your Faith Promise. Mark whether part or all of your offerings is an FP payment. Always sign the envelope.

Thank you again for your help in our effort to offer eternal life through Christ to people everywhere.

Sincerely,

Pastor John Doe

Figure 6

Include information in your bulletin as a regular bi-weekly feature like that illustrated below:

Faith Promise Update, August 11, (YEAR)

Promised weekly	Received on 8/11	Promised by 8/11	Total Received by 8/11	Long (or Short) by 8/11
$325	$355	$3,575	$3,691	+ 119

We have a balance of $119 in our mission account as shown for which we praise God!

Figure 7

Keep the congregation abreast on "Missions/Faith Promise" income. Work to be able to announce a positive balance in the missions account in order to encourage and motivate the congregation. The format above is effective as a bi-weekly bulletin feature. When the amount at the right shows "Long" give public praise. When "Short" exhort and pray for improvement. Seek ways to feature world outreach frequently as a top priority of your congregation.

Chapter 11

Questions Answered

Questions often asked include:

1. What is a Faith Promise?

A Faith Promise is a voluntary commitment a person makes to give a fixed amount of money to a church's missions budget within a year.

2. Is an FP the same as a pledge?

No, a pledge suggests an obligation between a giver and a church, whereas an FP emphasizes the relation between the giver and God. A pledge may be a legal obligation while an FP is not. No demanding letters are sent; no one is asked for his FP.

3. What is the purpose of FP?

FP's primary purpose is to raise the finances needed for the evangelization of the world.

4. Should every Christian be committed to world evangelization?

Yes, Christ commands it. See Matthew 28:18-20, Mark 16:15-16, Luke 24:45-48, etc.

5. Must FP funds come from a special source?

To insist that FP funds come from a special source limits Faith Promise. Funds from any honest origin are good if faith prompts the gift.

6. Is an FP bank account needed?

Yes, open an FP bank account that is separate from the church's general fund.

7. Should an FP goal be set for the missions budget?

Yes, the missions budget should be published at least a month before the annual conference. This enables people to pray about their FP.

8. What should a missions budget include to warrant sacrificial FPs?

A missions budget should include people and projects truly vital to world evangelization.

9. What about new projects?

New projects are great, but first review the budget from the previous year. As faith embraces new opportunities, include them, knowing that more and/or larger FPs will be needed.

10. When and how should FPs be received?

FPs should be received at the close of services on two or more Sundays, or at the close of the final meeting of the annual Missions Conference.Urge people to fill out and return an FP card. The sum of the total of these is then the missions budget for the coming year.

11. What if FPs total less than the goal that was set?

When FPs total less than the anticipated goal the missions budget will then have to be cut to equal the total available.

12. How are FP payments made?

Use offering envelopes with a 'Missions/Faith Promise' line that can be marked. (See illustration in chapter 10.) Make these envelopes available to all, teaching them to indicate on the outside of the envelope that the enclosed money is to fulfill their FP.

13. What percentage of FPs will be paid?

A well-led church will surpass its goal year after year. Some FPs may not be paid in full, however, gifts to the missions budget from individuals who made no FP will usually make up the amount.

14. What is the secret of FP success?

The pastor's enthusiastic support is essential to inspire faith and lead his people to victory. An FP Plan clothed in prayer is also a key to success.

15. What part does faith play in an FP?

Only the giver and God know. Faith is trust; faith always acts. A true FP stretches faith. Woody Phillips says, "It takes faith to sacrifice and refigure your budget because you have to believe that God will meet your needs with less money. It takes faith to be creative and find sources of funds you don't now see."

16. How can a church that gives a fixed percentage of its general fund to missions change to FP with two separate budgets?

To make change easy, explain it in advance. Suppose a church was giving 30% of its income to missions, explain that from the date of change only funds marked 'Missions/ Faith Promise' will go to missions. Thus, if a person was giving $100 per week to the church, missions got $30. To give the same he would make an FP of $30 per week; to give more he would increase his FP.

17. Should an FP be signed?

Yes, count only signed FPs. A church with missionaries in far places depending on them should know that it's FPs come from real people. Signing the cards solidifies the commitment, creates accountability, and helps will tax credits. Remember, Christ sat beside the treasury once and watched the people drop in their offerings, then commented on them (Mark 12:41-44). Something similar might be healthy today!

18. Should the total given to missions by FP be made public?

Why not? In Indiana a family read in the newspaper that a church was giving over $100,000 to missions. They could hardly believe it. Their church with a budget of several hundred thousand dollars was giving only $1,500 a year to missions. The family visited the other church and got excited about missions. They told four other families and later, together, bought a bicycle for a missionary. The next year, the five families revisited the church and together gave a wrist watch to a missionary. The pastor told me, "That was five years ago. This year those five families are giving $25,000 to missions!" From a bicycle to $25,000 in five years, and a news ad on missions giving started it all.

19. Will the FP Plan motivate Christians to give to missions?

Perhaps not, but it will increase the giving of those who are so motivated.

20. What kind of church will succeed with FP?

FP will cause a pastor and people who have a passion to assist world evangelization to do much more than they would otherwise do.

21. If using the FP Plan makes giving for missions go up, won't giving for local needs drop?

Amazingly, just the opposite is true. Paul Smith, whose church gives over two million dollars a year to missions says, "My experience through many years of FP giving for missions has been that as our missionary budget rises, our local income increases."

22. Are churches permanently pleased with the FP Plan?

Based on my experiences, yes. Some years ago I sent out a questionnaire and received back responses from 179 churches that had used the FP Plan. Some questions and their answers follow:

1. Has the FP Plan encouraged missionary candidates to go from your church? *51% said yes.*

2. Has the Plan helped in raising the support for the missionaries sent from your congregation? *62% said yes.*

3. Has it resulted in increased missionary giving? *93% said yes.*

4. Have local expenses suffered as a result of this Plan? *92% said no.*

5. Has giving for local expenses increased? *83% said yes.*

6. Do you feel you would do a service to other churches to encourage them to adopt the FP Plan to help evangelize the world? *96% said yes.*

Chapter 12

Receiving Faith Promises

Faith Promise is both a tool and a weapon for the Church at war. The objective is to plant churches in people groups who still have no knowledge of Christ. The powers of darkness will not withdraw without a fight.

President Theodore Roosevelt described "Mad Anthony" Wayne, a Brigadier at 34, as "the greatest field general America ever produced." During the Revolutionary War, while the British were encamped at Germantown, George Washington held one of his many councils of war. Wayne was all for attacking without delay but most of the other officers sat around the table offering innumerable excuses for holding back. When all the dissenting votes were in, Washington turned to Wayne, sitting quietly in a corner reading a book. "What would you say, General?" Wayne slammed the book shut, then rose slowly to his feet, glaring defiance at the group of distinguished officers. "I'd say nothing Sir. I'd fight."

Christians must fight to finish the Church's task of world evangelization. Your mission thrust is a part of the age-long battle to bring God's Son and his kingdom to earth. Every FP effort to support that aim strikes at evil. As you start any Sunday on which FPs are to be received, be aware that a day of battle has dawned. Make that day a high day in your church year.

Pastor, set the tone. Inspire the church to fight and

win. The FP Plan demands "doing" to dislodge the enemy. Christian stewards, your lives and possessions are assets you hold in trust for that purpose. Set your hearts to give all to gain that goal. Through FP giving win a victory for our Lord Jesus Christ.

Put a premium on prayerful, unified focused effort in meetings planned for receiving FPs. In many churches the day might develop like this. The pastor meets early with the Sunday School superintendent for prayer. They agree in their purpose to maximize Sunday School FP giving.

Next the pastor meets briefly with the ushers and the FP tally team. He may refer to special aspects of their work gathering and totaling FPs.

Just before the service the pastor joins his platform team. He emphasizes that every part of the program should encourage people to make an FP. He reminds them that only a true team effort in dependence on the Holy Spirit will maximize the making of FPs. They pray that the Word preached will motivate the congregation to act.

As the meeting starts the pastor will announce that its special purpose is to receive FPs to support the world's most important work. He might say: "Pray about your FP during this meeting and remember the standard Jesus set. Not what you give, but what you keep for yourself is the way God measures your giving (Mark 12:41 ff.). What we hold for ourselves may actually condemn us. Our Lord has told us it is more blessed to give than to receive. 'God loves a cheerful giver.' Faith believes God's Word and acts on it. Our giving to reach the unreached tests us deeply.

"How plainly our Lord Jesus pointed out the way we can please him when he said, 'I tell you, use worldly wealth to gain friends for yourselves, so that when it is gone, you will be welcomed into eternal dwellings' (Luke 16:9). What a day that will be in heaven when some of us meet those our gifts have won. So...pray, trust God, and obey him."

Make sure the pastor exhorts with an earnest, personal witness in favor of making an FP. The pastor's example and influence is of great importance as a model for his people.

Seek to make every part of the meeting support receiving FPs. A member of the platform team must keep the program on schedule even if parts must be shortened or cut. Before receiving the usual offering, remind the congregation that FPs will be received at the close of the meeting. The pre-sermon elements occupy a quarter of the time, the sermon half, and receiving the FP the last quarter. The common denominator of all elements of the program, however, is encouragement to make an FP. That is the act of obedience that validates one's profession of faith.

As the sermon ends, each usher is ready with FP cards cross-piled. They come quickly and each hand a pack of cards to the first person in each row. Everyone is asked to take a card, whether he expects to use it or not, in order to encourage those seated beside him. The speaker has the audience look at their cards while he reads the text aloud. He prays briefly that God will guide each giver, then asks that cards be filled in, signed, turned face down for privacy and passed to an aisle. The ushers then gather the cards and take them to the tally team.

The tally team is seated at a table close to the platform. The interpreter receives the FP cards from the ushers, verifies the signature, circles the weekly amount (or notes it based on data on the card), then passes the card to the adder. He enters the amount in the adding machine. The machine tape permits him to furnish sub-totals when asked in order for the thermometer column to be raised.

The speaker may ask for cards already recorded in order to read out amounts on several cards. This may be of help to people still undecided. Read only the weekly amount, never the name.

Maintain a sense of purpose during this period but avoid any overt pressure. When it is evident that most FPs are in, the leader may invite those who are still undecided to put God to the test by making a modest FP. To make a small FP is better than to do nothing. Anything that will nudge people toward more active trust in God will later bring them blessing and prompt them to exercise more faith in the future.

A chorus or two may be sung and brief comments made during this time, but the focus is kept on making FPs. When all have been counted, the thermometer column is moved up and the pastor announces the FP total. He closes the meeting with hearty thanksgiving to God and praise for his grace. FPs that support God's global program glorify God.

Chapter 13

Hold Missions High

Years ago I was in a church that had grown from a handful of people until their Faith Promise giving to missions was over $100,000 a year, at that time a huge sum. I asked the pastor how long it took to get ready for their annual missions conference. He said, "We start the Sunday after our conference closes." They kept world evangelization always at the top of their priorities. They were determined not to let their world vision diminish. A good goal to embrace.

When your annual missions event ends, send a letter promptly to encourage each person who made an FP. Note the model in Chapter 10. Confirm and commend the donor's act and explain how FP payments are made. Timing is important. Ready the letter for mailing the day after FPs are received. Send quickly, without fail, a letter to every person who made an FP.

While several matters in this chapter are not a part of the FP Plan itself, they make it stronger. Let FP giving be a vital element of a church climate charged with missions commitment.

Review for follow-up the names of all those who made public commitment or filled out a significant responseform during your missions event. Personal follow-up of such individuals should parallel the ongoing effort to hold high the profile of God's global cause. Both people and money are essential for world evangelization.

Invest in people who give evidence that God's Spirit is working in them. Take special pains to develop a meaningful relationship with people who are considering Christian service. Reach out with love and unselfish efforts to help them. Encourage them to move toward greater involvement in the world task. Personal follow-up is the difference between superficial and serious disciplemaking.

Plan ways to demonstrate that God's worldwide work is a true priority for your church. One pastor speaks of 'A firm and visionary administration'. He says, "Just because a project is called missions does not mean it merits support! Teach your elders, deacons, committees and congregation. Utilize panels, interviews, reports and other means to help your congregation to develop discernment."

Include practical insights and information on world evangelization in Sunday activities. Before receiving the offering the pastor might mention missions, and then say, "Why do you think the bible shows a weekly cycle of giving? Could it be that God wants us to think at least that often of giving to send the gospel to peoples still unreached?" Delegate people to gather for the pastor vital information and current anecdotes from missionaries the church supports. Announce such news often, include it in the bulletin, or make it a special insert.

A Los Angeles church placed the following notice in its bulletin about a month after its annual world outreach event:

> "To keep our FP giving practical, we
> are sharing with the body the facts. We need
> each week $3,564 to keep our people on the
> field. This is apart from designated giving.

"We must remind each other that we
are committed to at least 70 missionaries
through more than 30 missions who depend
on us each and every week. The best dollar we
ever spend is the one we send to a faithful
missionary. We will keep you posted as we go
along."

-From "Calvary Review".

Use the bulletin to keep the congregation current on
missions finances. Bi-weekly, show the year-to-date commitment and the actual income. If the balance is positive, praise
God. If not, encourage prayer. Encourage steady FP giving
by keeping the congregation informed about income for missions.

Make notes on your recent conference, with ideas for
improvement. It is easy to do so while memory is vivid. Edit
such notes once or twice, and then file them for future
reference. Open a file folder for "World Outreach Ideas" where
clippings and your notes can be kept. Seek names of effective
FP conference speakers. Contact your next speaker a year in
advance if possible.

Paul Josephson, a key lay worker for many years at
Black Rock Congregational Church knows the value of
planning ahead and working hard to depict the theme of a
Missions Conference. He writes, "We have put on some very
special theme presentations. The missions conference is the
key to setting the stage for the FP Plan. We bring on loads of
missionaries who do more in the homes of people than those
in the pulpit. We tell the missionaries that there will be little if
any pulpit time but we want them to minister to the needs in
the homes where they are guests. The results are many and
often spectacular. The missionaries in the pulpit are carefully

chosen, not to tell stories, but to share from the Word, the basis for missions. Stories are soon forgotten, but the Word remains forever in the hearts of the people."

Josephson also mentions with appreciation the availability of the Advancing Churches Missions Commitments (ACMC) representatives. This is the only organization of nationwide stature that exists for the sole purpose of helping church missions committees function more effectively. Affirm the importance of worldwide outreach for Christ by careful advanced planning and publicity.

God's plan for global redemption flows through the whole Bible. For two decades Pastor Verl Lindley of the Granada Heights Friends Church has kept the priority of world evangelization before his people. He says about his start, "I made a Faith Promise to see if it would work before I presented it to my church. From the very first month God demonstrated to me his faithfulness. The first year at our church our missionary giving increased from $19,000 to $52,000. Now it is in excess of $250,000. FP has prospered even when we have had building fund campaigns. We have found that FP leads to greater faith, prayer and generosity in all areas of the Lord's work.

"Increased missionary involvement has meant a steady flow of our people going to the mission field. Two of my daughters are now on the field. When FP is presented, not as a gimmick to raise money, but as a way of life, it works! I heartily recommend it. For several years it has had a profound effect on our people and their involvement in world outreach."

Leaders with vision head churches that grow. The whole Bible attests the prime relevance of God's redemptive purpose for the world. Give God's global goals priority in your church programs.

Chapter 14

Faith Promise Summarized

Faith Promise giving for world evangelization can make your church more effective for God. You need not "reinvent the wheel" to achieve real improvement. Benefit from things others have tested and proved. Believe God and build on the Bible. Here are some hints to help you:

Think of humanity's lostness and alienation from God. A Christless eternity is an awful reality. **Let the Bible's revelation of the fate of lost people move you to help evangelize the unreached with God's good news.**

Every Christian will agree the best thing he ever did was to receive Jesus Christ. Also that the best thing he can do for anyone else is to help him receive Christ. That effort, enlarged to global proportions, is world evangelization. **Involve yourself in the best business on earth, offering Christ to people everywhere.**

The Bible is the only bedrock on which to build a human life. Its central theme is God's purpose through his children to offer eternal life to people everywhere. **Embrace FP in order to support more effectively God's global redemptive purpose.**

With a separate missions budget, FP giving for missions can increase year by year without detriment to other church programs. To increase the percent of missions support in a unified budget, however, cuts the amount left for other church programs. That may offend people. Conflict may result. **Use the two budget FP Plan and church harmony is helped.**

Keep the FP Plan simple to make it easy for people to participate. Define "faith" as trust in God; "promise" as something you tell someone you will do. Describe FP giving in terms of its own intrinsic worth. **Define FP with utter simplicity for greatest success.**

Tell the congregation how much the missions budget is and how it will be used in order to enable people to pray intelligently about the amount of their FP. Show the congregation the importance of the church's commitment to world evangelization. **Present the missions budget as a major matter a month before your annual outreach event.**

People can be expected to make a costly FP only if they know its stated purpose merits sacrifice. Jesus taught that sinners who received him would be given eternal life, to refuse would mean death (Mk. 16:16). **Explain that to make an FP may bring people from death to eternal life.**

People sometimes ask what percent of a church's FP total will be paid? Answer "The full amount will come in." They may protest, "That's not reasonable." I explain that while some FPs may not be paid, the "Missions/FP" option on the offering envelope invites gifts from people who have not made an FP. They will make up the lack. Base the missions budget on the total FPs received. **The church can expect to receive a sum equal to the FP total.**

Suppose a church has been giving 20% of its income to missions, and then decide to adopt FP. Explain that anyone who wants his giving to missions to stay the same should make his FP for 20% of what he formerly gave each week. If he gave $100 a week before, $20 went to missions. If he now makes a Faith Promise of $20 a week, his giving to missions stays the same. If he wants to give more to missions, he makes a larger FP. **An advantage of FP giving is that each donor, as he is led, can adjust his giving between local needs and missions.**

Ask that all FP cards be signed to attest to their validity. Anonymous numbers mean little as the basis for a church financial commitment. The problem is serious when the amount given to missions is significant. Grantd that God can interpret an unsigned car, yet on the human level a signature gives meaning. Though some believe unsigned cards are best, it seems wise to ask donors to sign their cards. **Tell the congregation that only signed FP cards will be counted.**

It is sometimes asserted that to make public the amount a congregation gives to missions is unspiritual. Many cases could be certified, however, in which people have been drawn to a church and inspired to give because they were impressed by the amount of money a congregation was giving to missions. **Give glory to God and information to the public about the amount of money given to missions.**

When a church adopts the FP Plan, announce that Missions/FP on the offering envelope marks the sole channel for missions support. Don't keep the old system in place as a "help" to FP. **On the last date set to receive FPs, move all mission support to the new plan.**

It has been argued that what man can picture in his mind he can achieve. It is certain that to clearly envision goals, aids in reaching them. The more vividly you visualize FP succeeding in your church, the more surely it will do so. **Picture the whole FP Plan functioning in your church.**

An FP is usually made for twelve months. Dates to receive FPs rarely coincide with the start of the calendar year or the church fiscal year. Someone may suggest delaying FP payments until one of those times. No, to postpone payments on FPs would be very unwise. When the missions event closes and the spirit of giving it high, start. **Encourage donors to make FP payments the very Sunday after FPs have been received.**

Print the Missions/FP option on the offering envelope for at least three good reasons: It affirms that missions is important. It assists accurate record keeping. It encourages all believers to give to missions. **Be sure the Missions/FP option appears on your offering envelope.**

Always take pains to investigate in advance the speaker for your missions event. Make sure he can explain clearly the Biblical basis for missions and the FP Plan. It is good for the pastor to receive FPs, but people must first be motivated from the Word of God. **Get speakers gifted in presenting the Biblical basis for world evangelization and the FP Plan.**

Encourage open enthusiasm favoring a budget poster and thermometer. These tools dramatize an important idea. They give the FP goal a special look and help make it come alive. **Use a huge poster and thermometer to dramatize the missions financial goal.**

Any meeting to receive FPs should focus primarily on that act of personal obedience. Make every part of the program contribute to the final result. Ask of every element, "Does it motivate to real commitment?" Persuasion is in order for the motive is right. Hold the pre-message segment to 25 percent of the meeting. Make time for the Holy Spirit to apply the truth of the message to hearts. **In every meeting to receive FPs, focus every part of the program on encouraging people to make an FP.**

Hold heartily the conviction that the splendor of the FP Plan is its use to support the most important task on earth, to evangelize the world with the good news of salvation through our Lord Jesus Christ. **The FP Plan will strengthen your congregation's purpose to be ambassadors for Christ to earth's unreached people groups.**

Chapter 15

Faith Promise Is For Life

The Faith Promise Plan encourages believers to pray. When Vince Lombardi began as coach of the Green Bay Packers, he said, "I've never been with a losing team in my life and I don't think I'll start now." The first day he took over the Packers, Lombardi told the team, "Gentlemen, we're going to have a football team. We're going to win some games. Do you know why? Because you're going to have confidence in me and my system."

In a higher realm the FP Plan inspires confidence in the God who commands us to make disciples among all nations (Matt 28:18). He sends us to the work and he will supply the resources we need. FP can greatly aid us in doing what God wants done. It strengthens support for the noblest cause on earth (John 3:17). It enables people to give more than they otherwise would. FP supports the purpose of Christ, "I give them eternal life" (John 10:28).

I led an FP missions conference in a church two successive years. After the second series, a man wrote me saying, "In the fall a year ago, I signed a Faith Promise to pay a weekly sum to missions. In spite of inflation and other adverse conditions, this has been the best year of my twenty years in the garage business. I intend to double my FP in the coming year."

After an FP conference in Montana, the following

letter came from a salesman. "I promised the Lord I would
give $20 a week if he would send it in. The rest of this you will
find almost impossible to believe. My commissions, instead of
averaging $225 per week which is normally good, have run
over $1,000 per week ever since this shaky and trembling
commitment was made to the Lord."

An FP conference in California brought me a letter
which said: "My income is dependent on sales of musical
merchandise in my store." The writer then mentions having
left teaching in order to try to earn more money for missions.
He continues, "The first day in business we asked a missionary to pray a prayer of dedication of our business to God.
What a prayer! He suggested a Faith Promise of $25 a week
more than our regular giving. This overwhelmed us, but we
said, 'Yes.' We had never given that much money to God in
our lives!

" Guess what? The first day in business we had $200.
The first year in business I almost tripled my teaching salary.
In the last ten or twelve years we have been privileged to
redirect over $50,000 to God's work throughout the world.
The more I did this, the more God saw fit to trust me with.
I've never outgiven God. I believe such a thing is impossible."

Missionaries themselves tell of blessings through FP
giving: "The Faith Promise concept we heard night after night
finally sank in. FP means to trust God to channel his resources
through a person. There was a debt on headquarters and we
missionaries were told, 'If we each ask God for a thousand
dollars the debt can be wiped out this year.' So we made a
$2,000 FP. A few days later we were amazed to receive $500
from our home church. So immediately we have $500 for our
FP.

"That was in March. By the end of May the Lord had

provided a total of $1360 for the project. During that time our savings account for our family needs increased from $5 to over $1,000. Though we expected the Lord to provide the $2,000 by the end of the year, we had more than that by September. We thank God for honoring the eagerness he gave us to be a channel for his resources."

Thousands of people are committed to FP because it has brought them blessing. It has proved to them that God is faithful. They will practice FP giving as long as they live. FP is for life.

Countless churches have experienced an explosion of their giving for overseas witness since they embraced the FP Plan. Their outpouring of money across the years seems a miracle to many people. Volunteers for God's vital task of worldwide witness appears simultaneously in many churches as added assets become available for their support. People's lives tend to follow Spirit-led liberality in giving. Our Lord said, "Where your treasure is, there will your heart be also" (Matt 6:21).

Churches that have implemented FP giving success-fully make worldwide witness for Christ their permanent major thrust. The Adopt-A-People program of the U.S. Center for World Mission is an invaluable resource. Churches are study-ing unreached people. Teams are being formed to penetrate groups with no church. Such congregations are pacesetters for others who will follow their example. The aim is to give God's good news to all people groups who lack it.

Churches that focus their giving on Christless people develop world Christians. They attract generous people. Unselfish giving is always winsome. A church about it's Master's business is at its best. FP giving aids a church's image and enhances it reputation. Congregations that achieve such results will continue FP giving to achieve the goal God has given. In churches that know the difference this method has made, FP is for life.

Suppose we could assemble the testimony of all the churches which use the FP Plan with success. They would still be but a modest minority of evangelical churches. Do their successes give grounds for self-congratulations? Shall even our best churches boast? Let us look at the larger picture of God's plan and purpose. He has given his people global goals. Only our commitment in reaching them will please God.

This book does not aim at self-commendation nor is the FP Plan a panacea for poor performance. The Western Church has erred grievously from God's plan. Most churches are far off target, majoring on minors.

We have not focused on offering everyone on earth a reasonable chance to know Jesus Christ (John 17:3).

We have not made it our main business to "go into all the world and preach the good news to all creation" (Mark 16:15).

We have not loved the Lord our God with all our heart, soul, and mind, and our neighbors as ourselves (Matt. 22:37-39).

We have not paid the price to be our brother's keeper (Genesis 4:9).

We have not honored our role as children of Abraham by fulfilling God's Word that "all peoples on earth will be blessed through you" (Genesis 12:3).

We have not made it our priority to "declare his glory among the nations, his marvelous deeds among all peoples" (Psalm 96:3).

We have not made it our aim to fulfill the promise that "all the ends of the earth shall see how our God saves" (Isaiah 52:10).

We have not made Christ's prophecy become history, for he said, "This gospel must first be published among the nations" (Mark 13:11).

We have not given first place to Christ's words that, "Repentance and forgiveness of sins will be preached in his name to all nations" (Luke 24:47).

We have not honored in spirit or letter Christ's words, "as the Father has sent me, I am sending you" (John 20:21).

We have not imitated Christ's example when he said, "I must preach the good news of the kingdom of God to the other towns also, because that is why I was sent" (Luke 4:43).

We have not obeyed Christ's guidance, "You will be my witnesses in Jerusalem, and in all Judea, and Samaria, and to the ends of the earth" (Acts 1:8).

We have not demonstrated that, "They who live should no longer live for themselves, but for him who died and rose for them" (2 Cor. 5:15).

We have not imitated Jesus' affirmation, "My food is to do the will of him who sent me and to finish his work" (John 4:34).

Nor have we embraced with passion Christ's prophecy that "this gospel of the kingdom must be preached in all the world for a witness to all nations and then the end shall come" (Matt. 24:14).

For such failure we must repent and make amends. Our restitution must continue until our world task is finished. Our lives must be lived to that end, our assets empower that enterprise, our minds solve the problems of that work. Our prayers must prevail with God for that cause, our hearts hold to gaining that goal, terminating that task.

A program that moves with God will merit his approval. As we do his work we will find his favor and hear at last his words, "well done, good and faithful servant...enter into the joy of our Lord" (Matt. 25:21).

This simple plan will result in rewards here and hereafter. It is linked to the unalterable purpose of our Lord who said, "I have come that they may have life" (John 14:10). Knowing that Faith Promise is for life, use the FP Plan to offer life in Christ worldwide - life eternal.